春
雪 Snow Falling in Spring

COMING OF AGE IN CHINA DURING THE CULTURAL REVOLUTION

MOYING LI

Snow Falling in Spring

COMING OF AGE IN CHINA DURING THE CULTURAL REVOLUTION

MELANIE KROUPA BOOKS

FARRAR, STRAUS AND GIROUX   NEW YORK

Snow Falling in Spring is a work of nonfiction. Some names and identifying details have been changed, and conversations and events are, of necessity, reconstructions based on the author's memory.

Text copyright © 2008 by Moying Li
Calligraphy by Gao Xiang
All rights reserved
Printed in the United States of America
Distributed in Canada by Douglas & McIntyre Ltd.
Designed by Irene Metaxatos
First edition, 2008
10 9 8 7 6 5 4 3 2 1

www.fsgkidsbooks.com

Library of Congress Cataloging-in-Publication Data
Li, Moying, date.
    Snow falling in spring : coming of age in China during the cultural revolution /
Moying Li.— 1st ed.
        p.   cm.
    ISBN-13: 978-0-374-39922-1
    ISBN-10: 0-374-39922-0
    1. Li, Moying, 1954– —Juvenile literature. 2. China—History—Cultural
Revolution, 1966–1976—Personal narratives—Juvenile literature.   I. Title.

DS778.7.L51155 2006
951.05′6—dc22
[B]

                                                                        2006038356

Photograph credits: page 5, Wang Wenbo; pages 131 and 132, Yu Chunze. All other
photographs are from the author's collection of family photographs.

To Grandma, Lao Lao, my guardian angel—
I dedicate this book

春思

雪罷枝即青
冰開水復綠
復聞黃鳥聲
全作相思曲

－王僧孺

南朝梁

Spring Remembrance

When snow stops falling,

Leaves turn green.

When ice melts away,

Water glistens blue.

Once again, the yellow bird chirps,

All sing a song of memories.

—Wang Sengru,
   a poet from the Southern (Liang) Dynasties,
   sixth century

Contents

Foreword

hirty years have passed since the end of the Cultural Revolution, but that dramatic time, and the many historical events leading up to it, still feel so close, so personal. My grandma, Lao Lao, was born at the turn of the twentieth century in Beijing, the ancient capital of China. It was called Beiping (Peiping) then, meaning "Peace in the North." There was, however, anything but peace when she was growing up. At that time, China was ravaged by war, and the government in Beiping changed hands many times—from the last imperial dynasty to the first republic. Even after the Republic of China was founded in 1912, warlords jockeyed for power, creating a situation so chaotic that, Lao Lao told me, it was hard to tell who was fighting whom.

The chaos worsened when, in 1931, the Japanese invaded the northeastern provinces of China and soon after installed a puppet regime under the last emperor, Pu Yi. In 1937, when Japanese troops attacked Lugouqiao—what was known to the

Western world as Marco Polo Bridge—twenty miles southwest of the capital, fighting escalated into a nationwide war. Eight more years of bloody combat against the Japanese ensued, led by the combined forces of the Nationalists, under Chiang Kai-shek, and the Communists, under Mao Zedong.

At the age of fourteen, my father, Baba, joined the fight against the Japanese invaders, first as a student in Beiping with the underground resistance, then, at fifteen, as a soldier. Finally, after China's victory over Japan, the fragile alliance between the Communists and the Nationalists fell apart, leading to four years of civil war between these two former allies. Baba fought on the side of the Communists. And they won. In 1949, when Chairman Mao announced to the world the founding of the People's Republic of China, Baba marched into the ancient capital among the liberating troops. For the first time, he believed that we, the Chinese people, had become the masters of our own destiny.

In 1958, the government, led by Chairman Mao, launched the Great Leap Forward. By mobilizing energy and enthusiasm from every corner of Chinese society, the leaders believed we could catch up with the West in just ten to twenty years—in a single giant stride. As a four-year-old, even I was affected by this unbridled exuberance. But instead of a "great leap," what we experienced was three years of natural and human calamity, when crops were destroyed by drought and insects and millions of people died of starvation.

Almost immediately following these catastrophes, another

wave, in 1966, hit us like an unstoppable tsunami and lasted for ten long years—a period when I grew from a young teenager to an adult. What struck us had a name. It was called the Great Proletarian Cultural Revolution.

Initially the Cultural Revolution was an attempt by Chairman Mao to get rid of his political enemies. But soon the "ocean waves" he set in motion gained a momentum of their own and wrecked everything in their path. From age twelve to twenty-two, I, along with over a billion other Chinese, was caught up in this overwhelming force. Even thirty years after its passing, I still, from time to time, feel its impact. My life, together with the lives of one-fifth of the world's population, was changed and shaped by this experience. And whether I like it or not, it will be part of me forever.

Prologue

It took me over twenty years to return to my grandma Lao Lao's old courtyard in Beijing, where I spent much of my short childhood. I was shocked to find it gone. Bulldozed. Wiped from the face of the earth. It was like discovering that a dear friend had died and realizing I had been robbed of the last chance to say goodbye.

I sat on a pile of shattered gray bricks—the only remnants of my grandpa Lao Ye's labor—watching the brisk November wind lift the withered leaves from the dusty ground, up and up and away from me.

Then I closed my eyes—to remember.

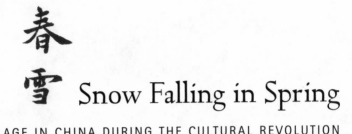

春雪 Snow Falling in Spring

COMING OF AGE IN CHINA DURING THE CULTURAL REVOLUTION

大躍進

The Great Leap

T WAS A HOT SUMMER, AND THE WORDS ON EVERY GROWNUP'S LIPS WERE *GREAT LEAP FOR-WARD*. "IN FIFTEEN YEARS," SOMEONE SAID, BUB-bling with excitement, "China will overtake Britain!" Then, Baba (Father) spun the wooden globe next to his desk and pointed out to me where Britain was. Touching the spot with my finger-tip, I murmured, "But it's so small." I could not understand why Baba and his friends were eager for China, a large splash of green on Baba's globe, to surpass another country that was only a gray speck—smaller than some Chinese provinces. But the glow of hope on their faces and the confidence in their voices told me that this Great Leap Forward would be a big accom-plishment—something to be truly proud of. I trusted grownups in those days with all my heart. This was the summer of 1958, and I was four years old.

My family lived in Beijing with my maternal grandmother, Lao Lao, and maternal grandfather, Lao Ye, in a traditional *si-*

heyuan—a large square yard surrounded by one-story houses with sloping roofs on each side. Sharing our *siheyuan* were my aunts and uncles and a few tenants: the families of a tailor, an electrician, and a clerk.

Decades before I was born, it was Lao Ye who carefully lined our roofs with smooth gray tiles and installed large windows along the brick walls. Above the glass windows were wooden *zhichuang* (shutters), which could be propped up by thin sticks to let in fresh air. When thunder and lightning raged outside, I would huddle with Lao Lao and watch it through the window-panes as she pampered me with sweet tea and cookies. Inside, I felt safe and cozy.

The garden in our courtyard was my favorite place, with flowers taking turns to blossom even into late fall. Our golden daffodils—or water fairies, as Lao Lao called them—proudly announced the coming of spring. In the summer, pale jasmine opened up at night, filling our *siheyuan* with its fragrance. Lao Lao encouraged the jasmine's nimble vines to climb freely up and around our bamboo fence, forming a blooming wall that separated the garden from the rest of the yard. Hardy chrysan-themums—in pink, yellow, and white—flowered from season to season. It was in this garden, I was told, that I took my first steps, surrounded by aunts and uncles, their arms reaching out to catch me if I fell.

Next to the jasmine wall was a tall *huaishu* (scholar tree). During the summer months, the sweet scent from its delicate flowers filled our yard, while the droning songs of cicadas, shel-

An old courtyard in Beijing

tered among its abundant leaves, lulled me to sleep. Under the *huaishu's* cooling shade, Lao Lao set up a permanent place for two of my favorite things—a little red wooden table and a small red armchair—gifts from my future uncle-in-law, who had lavished his craftsman's talent on me in a skillful pursuit of my doting aunt.

During the day, the garden became the center of our family activities, a place where the women sewed and washed, while the men chatted. For my brother, Di Di, and me, the large open yard next to the garden was both playground and battlefield. There, we shared our new tricycle with our neighbors' children, taking turns racing from one end of the yard to the other. Even though Di Di was a year younger than I, he was faster on the tricycle.

With our friend Ming, the tailor's youngest son, hanging on to the rear rack, Di Di would pedal past every door in our courtyard, waving to anyone who cared to look. Sometimes, the two of them would charge straight at me and the other girls until we screamed and scattered. In this big yard, grownups watched us from every window, but we felt totally free.

After a family dinner spread on a large square table, spiced by my uncles' jokes and my aunties' laughter, each family unit would retreat to its separate rooms. For me, however, there were no boundaries as I happily darted in and out of my parents' and grandparents' houses. Family was just family, I believed, without doors or walls. And as the first grandchild, I felt entitled to all of their hearts as well as their space.

Our farm animals were almost as free, housed in a shed under a giant elm tree in a corner of the courtyard. To me, the shed was like a small zoo. Two white rabbits with big red eyes lived there, as well as a rooster with glistening golden feathers, and four chickens—two white and two brown. Lao Lao had handpicked each animal from street vendors. The rabbits were my favorites, so warm and soft to the touch. Sometimes I even lured them into my bedroom with a carrot so that I could cuddle them.

ဢ

Early that summer when I was four, Baba took Di Di and me to visit his youngest sister, who lived by the sea. When we returned in the fall, I could hardly believe my eyes—our courtyard was strewn with bricks, holes, and scrap metal! An ugly brick furnace, almost as tall as Baba, stood right in the center. I was in shock.

"This is to make iron and steel for the Great Leap Forward," Baba said. "Our country needs strong construction materials."

That Great Leap again, I thought, remembering Baba's globe with its colorful dots and splashes. I stepped gingerly around my shattered yard, dodging the busy grownups who, shovels in hand, were too preoccupied to pay me the usual attention. Even Lao Lao joined their efforts. "Isn't it wonderful?" She beamed, holding me up in her arms. "We are helping our country."

"Yes, I know. We are going to catch up with that *small* dot before I grow up," I grumbled. Looking at what this Great Leap had done to my playground, I found it hard to share their excitement.

Soon my freedom, together with that of our rabbits and rooster, was restricted. Under Lao Lao's order, we were to stay in the garden behind the bamboo fence. Outside the fence, the world was pouring into our yard, day and night. Excited neighbors, scores of them, brought in firewood by the cartload and piled it up next to the furnace, ample fuel for the fire that crackled and roared. Some of the wood had been freshly split from old benches and chairs, with peeling paint and pointy nails still sticking out. The furnace, my enemy number one, was built with layers and layers of red bricks. On top of them sat a shiny metal hat with spurts of smoke, sometimes even red sparks, bursting out from under it. Fascinated but scared, I stared at the burning furnace, hugging my favorite rabbit for comfort.

None of this seemed to bother the grownups. They filed into our courtyard with their metal pots and pans—anything they could find and everything they could spare—to be melted into steel. People did not have much in those days, but the odds and ends soon looked like a small mountain next to the wood-pile. As I watched, the tailor's wife stepped out of her house with a frying pan. She hesitated, flipping the pan in her hands and wiping it again and again with her handkerchief. She seemed to be saying goodbye to an old friend.

Slowly, she walked up to the metal pile and gently laid her frying pan, now gleaming in the sun, on top of the little moun-tain. She stared at it for a few moments, then suddenly turned and walked away, never looking back.

Da Jiu (oldest maternal uncle), a math professor home on sick leave, was in charge of quality control. Stooping down from his slender height, he inspected the pile, separating the usable pieces from the junk. Picking up a wok cover, he examined it, tapped on it lightly, and then tossed it onto a smaller pile of re-jects. He nodded at the mountain of metal that was growing larger by the hour.

My favorite neighbor, Uncle Liu, the electrician, tall and broad-shouldered, stood by the furnace like a warrior, shoveling logs and broken chairs into its mouth. Gripping a long steel pole with both hands, he used its tip to hook open the hinges of the furnace door. He prodded the burning wood and then slapped the door shut when the wood started to crackle. It looked to me as if he was feeding a roaring dragon. The clerk, short and dark but equally solemn, used a large iron ladle to channel the red burning liquid into a mold, while our third neighbor, his face glowing from the heat of the flames, inspected the fruit of their labors with a tailor's precision.

Standing at a safe distance, I became transfixed by the scene in front of me and forgot about my fear and my destroyed playground. Then, an idea hit me. I bolted into Lao Lao's kitchen, threw open her large cabinet doors, and crawled on hands and knees in search of family treasure. I spotted a big water ladle at one corner of the cabinet and some spoons in a drawer, and threw them all into a bamboo basket next to the stove. I grabbed a large kettle and dropped it into the basket as well. Before darting outside, I surveyed the kitchen one last time and then threw Lao Lao's heavy cleaver on top of my prizes. Dragging the basket behind me, I hurried as fast as my feet and the load would allow and dumped everything, basket and all, onto the mound of metal carefully selected by Da Jiu. Thank goodness I had been watching closely and knew which pile was the chosen one!

I crept back behind the bamboo fence and slumped down in my little red chair, tired but satisfied. Throughout the day I sat there, spellbound. I shared every sign of triumph—the electrician patting the clerk's shoulder, the clerk shaking the tailor's hand, and then all of them giving a thumbs-up to Da Jiu. As the sun slowly set, leaving a trail of purple clouds in the crisp autumn sky, Da Jiu pushed his black-rimmed eyeglasses up and beamed.

Suddenly I heard Lao Lao's voice. She had just returned

At age four, in Lao Lao's courtyard, I'm ready to help

home, ready to tackle dinner. "Where is my kettle?" she asked, walking over to where I was sitting. "Have you seen my cleaver?"

"Yes, I helped our country with it," I replied proudly, without removing my eyes from the furnace. "Maybe they are burning it now."

Lao Lao rushed over to Da Jiu and his metal pile. Together, they found the kettle and some spoons, but not the big cleaver. The knife had joined its comrades in the burning fire, doing its share for China.

My escapade circulated around the dinner table that night. Choking from chewing and laughing at the same time, Baba turned to me and said, "It's good that you want to help, but next time it would be best to check with Lao Lao first."

ᔑ

Our roaring furnace popped and burned day and night for months. Every morning at dawn, our courtyard came alive with clatter and chattering. Then one morning I woke up to silence. Something was different. I ran outside to see.

In the courtyard, Da Jiu and our neighbors sat on the woodpile, their heads bowed like those of defeated soldiers. The fire in the furnace had died, leaving a lingering smell of burnt wood.

"What happened, Da Jiu?"

"The iron and steel we made was not good enough." He sighed. I stared at him in disbelief. "We simply did not know enough to make it right," he added.

Now I was sad, too. Climbing up the woodpile to sit next to him, I leaned my head against his shoulder, as crestfallen as he and our neighbors.

"But we tried so hard."

"Yes," he said. "We did."

For days, we all avoided the courtyard. The abandoned red furnace stood in the center, alone and silent, along with a few scattered metal pieces and some half-burnt wood. We all tiptoed around it as if we were visiting a patient in the hospital. From time to time, I would find myself resting my chin against the bamboo fence and staring at my soundless enemy turned old friend, silently wishing him to roar for me one more time. But he only stared back.

For weeks, Lao Lao refused to replace her cleaver and used a small knife instead. It was not the money for a new cleaver that stopped her, even though nobody had much to spare. It was the principle. Our big knife had sacrificed itself for a cause and so should be honored. At least that was my interpretation. The roaring furnace, too, had done his best, even though his best was not good enough.

Finally, the furnace disappeared, and so did the scattered

wood and metal. The men filled the holes in the yard with fresh dirt, and Lao Lao swept the courtyard clean. I was free once again to race my tricycle with Di Di and my friends, and spend quiet moments smelling the flowers and petting my rabbits. In our garden, the women resumed their sewing and washing, and the men their chatting. Life seemed to have gone back to what it was before.

But, then, why did I feel as if something had changed?

Starvation

HOTS FROM BABA'S PELLET GUN SLICED THROUGH THE COOL SPRING NIGHT. I LOOKED UP AND HELD MY BREATH. THE DARK SHADOW OF A SPARROW hit our rooftop and then tumbled down, landing in our garden with a soft thud.

"Hurrah!" Di Di and I shouted. Together with a dozen other children from our neighborhood, we scrambled to pick up Baba's prey.

For some time now, sparrows had been officially condemned as one of the *sihai* (four evils)—joining the ranks of rats, mosquitoes, and flies. While rats infested our houses, the government claimed, sparrows destroyed our crops. In 1958, the year of the Great Leap Forward, China declared war on these *sihai*, and we were instructed to wipe them out from our entire land within the next few years.

Now, every neighborhood had been turned into a war zone. Morning and night, grownups took turns standing guard in our courtyard. As soon as the sparrows landed on trees or rooftops, these watchful guards would drive them away with a loud whistle or an accurate and merciless stone.

Baba, with his pellet gun, had earned everyone's respect as an excellent shot. Di Di and I followed him everywhere. As soon as he raised the barrel of his gun and aimed, I felt my muscles tighten and my head perk up like that of a puppy on its first hunt.

During the day, the three teenage sons of Uncle Liu turned our elm tree into a watchtower, warning everyone within shouting distance of incoming enemies. At night, Baba, my uncles, and other grownups took over, with searchlights fastened onto the rooftops, leaving no dark corner for the birds to hide in.

Not to be outdone by the adults, Di Di, our friends, and I put our heads together to come up with our own ideas. Someone suggested that we use our washbasins as gongs, and we all rushed to our houses and came back with ceramic basins, tin cans, metal rice bowls, and spoons. Lining up, we marched around the courtyard, banging on our makeshift weapons like members of a dissonant percussion orchestra.

From time to time, we would also go patrolling on our *hutong* (lane), running from one end to the other and pounding our weapons as loud as we could. Grownups might have their lofty ideas, but to me it was simply fun. No one, not even Lao Lao, bothered to remind me of bedtime anymore. For several nights I stayed up well past midnight. Other than not touching Baba's pellet gun, I was free to pursue anything I liked, and I liked nothing better than running and making noise with my friends. Often Di Di and I shared meals with them, and later we would all fall asleep together in a friendly heap.

Soon, however, Lao Lao took away my metal rice bowl and Di Di's tin can—her ears were ringing with all the noise we had created. After losing our little percussion group, we each found the best spot we could and watched, not wanting to miss anything. At first, Di Di and I stood on stools we had lifted onto our red wooden table. But this vantage point was still too low.

"How about climbing on top of that?" Di Di whispered, pointing at our chicken coop.

Normally, I wouldn't even have considered doing this, knowing how much Lao Lao cared for her animals. On the other hand, I thought, it probably was the tallest place we could reach. I nodded to Di Di, and we quietly carried our stools over and stacked them up. Carefully, feeling like an acrobat, I climbed on the stools and up onto the top of the wooden shack. Then I leaned over and pulled Di Di up. No one noticed us; they were all preoccupied with our common enemy—the sparrows.

And so, day after day we watched the battle unfold as vigilant Beijingers stood their ground. Then, suddenly, sparrows started to fall from the sky, utterly exhausted. Soon there were hardly any left. At dinner one evening, flushed with pride as he waved a copy of the *People's Daily*, Baba announced that in our city alone we had eradicated over 400,000 sparrows!

"We won, we won!" I shouted. Our crops would be safe.

But the very next year, acres and acres of rice and wheat died anyway, this time destroyed by insects that had multiplied easily because their natural predators—the sparrows—had failed to return.

That was just the beginning. During the next three years, China suffered disaster after disaster. In addition to the plague of insects, there was a terrible drought, followed by widespread famine. Millions of people died of starvation. In the city, our food was strictly rationed. We had tiny coupons for everything—wheat, rice, cooking oil, and meat. Lao Lao tried to go to the food store regularly, but more often than not, the store would run out of supplies. As a first grader, I had my lunch at school, and for weeks, we had been eating rice and fruit jam every single day. Pretty soon, my belly started to churn at the very sight of rice with jam.

"I hate the sour rice at school," I grumbled to Lao Lao one day. "May I have lunch at home?"

With a sad look on her face, she bent down and wrapped her arms around me. "We are all going through hard times," she said. It did not take me long to realize how silly I was to complain.

With most grownups in my family working outside the city during the week, Lao Lao now cooked just for Lao Ye, Di Di, and me. I began to notice that she would make dinner for Di Di and me, watch us eat, and then quickly send us out to play in the yard before she cooked for herself and Lao Ye. At first, I did not think much about this, but one day I smelled the difference—the aroma coming from their meal was strange. When Lao Lao wasn't looking, I lifted the wok cover to discover grayish water with some vegetable leaves floating on top. Earlier that night, my brother and I had eaten rice and stir-fried cabbage, complete with a spoonful of meat. I ran to share the discovery with Di Di. The next day, we threatened a hunger strike unless Lao Lao allowed us to eat exactly the same thing they ate.

"But you two are still growing and need more nutrition," she said with a sigh. "We are old now and can do without it."

No! This time it was Di Di and I who stood our ground.

∽

For days now, Lao Lao had been circling her little animal farm, looking at her chickens and patting her rabbits—all of which had grown thinner, since their rations were reduced as well. I sensed something was about to happen. Finally, coming back from school one late afternoon, I was overwhelmed by mouthwatering smells. I ran to the chicken coop and threw open the gate; the rooster was missing. Even though I had never been fond of that rooster, I could not help but feel sad for him.

Also attracted to the fragrant aroma was my friend Ming, the youngest of the tailor's five children. Small and thin, he stood outside our garden, his hands resting on the bamboo fence, and stared at our kitchen.

"Come, dear," Lao Lao called, and I ran in. "Go give this bowl of chicken soup to Ming."

Carefully, I carried a big porcelain bowl filled to the brim with meat and broth to my friend. "Don't spill it," I cautioned him.

Even more gingerly, he inched away, clutching the bowl

tightly with both hands, stopping halfway to nod a thank-you to me. Quite often, he would find his way to our garden at dinner-time, attracted by the cooking smells. Each time, Lao Lao would pull up a chair next to me and sit him down, adding a fresh rice bowl and a pair of chopsticks to the table. "We'll make it," she would say. "We'll make it together."

Our animal population dwindled quickly, until one day all the chickens and rabbits were gone. That afternoon, with a large broom in her hand, Lao Lao went to clean the chicken coop one last time. Nobody said anything. We knew how much she had loved her animals. Picking up a small broom, I joined her, and together we swept in silence.

One morning, weeks after we had closed down the chicken coop, I was suddenly jolted awake. I cursed the rooster under my breath, thinking I had his crowing to blame. But rubbing my eyes, I remembered the rooster was gone. What I'd heard were voices coming from the yard.

Hurrying out, I saw Lao Lao under the big elm tree talking to a neighbor from the adjacent courtyard. Hanging on to one of the branches, her older boy was shaking the tree to make the leaves fall, and her two young girls were picking up the leaves and putting them in a basket.

I went over to where Lao Lao was standing and took her hand. Our neighbor was explaining that she could mix these leaves with corn flour to make corn bread. I picked up a leaf and put it in my palm to examine it. It was round and flat with a soft center. Could these leaves feed people? Bowing to Lao Lao, our neighbors left, their basket overflowing.

"They are more in need than we are," Lao Lao said, patting me on the head.

Before dinner, our neighbor reappeared—this time carrying three steaming loaves of leafy corn bread. "Try it," she said. I took a bite. It tasted a little bitter—like some herbal medicine Lao Lao had given me.

"Come back anytime if you need more," said Lao Lao.

"Thank you, Mama," she answered, with a grateful smile.

Everybody—my parents, my aunts, uncles, and their friends, as well as our neighbors—seemed to call Lao Lao "Mama." I remember feeling left out when I was little and begging that I be allowed to call her Mama, too.

"Sorry," Lao Lao had said, laughing. "I am your grandma."

Unsatisfied, one day I asked a friend of Da Jiu, whom I also called Uncle, "How come you can call Lao Lao 'Mama' but I can't?"

Sitting me down on his lap, he looked me in the eye and said, "Because my mother died when I was younger than you, and your *lao lao* took me in. She fed me, dressed me, and loved me the same as she did your blood uncle, my best friend. To me she has become the mama I lost a long time ago. And I am not the only one. Uncle Lin is also an orphan and, as you know, he grew up here as part of your family, too."

I had no idea. I had never questioned the many, many people I called Uncle and Auntie. All of them were here when I came into this world, and all of them took turns caring for me, bringing me candies and reading me bedtime stories. I lost track of how many people ate and slept in Lao Lao's house. To me, they were *all* my family. And during the time of the famine, they all managed, somehow, to send us food coupons and money so that we did not starve.

∽

By 1962 three disastrous years had finally passed. We had survived the Great Leap, the drought, and the starvation. But the grownups seemed to have lost some of their exuberance. They were still eager for their causes, but a hint of caution was added to their voices. One day after dinner, I pulled my wooden stool up next to Baba as he sat chatting with our extended family. Someone pointed to where the big furnace used to be, while another chuckled with embarrassment at how excited we had been when the sparrows started to fall. Looking up at Baba's face, I thought I saw him wince.

"Ignorance," Baba said. "That's our enemy. In the future we need to educate ourselves."

Recently Baba had brought home piles of new books, all thick and solemn-looking. Even as a child, I could tell that his attitude had changed from his cheerful confidence in the fall of 1958, when the brick furnace had burned happily in our yard. Seeing the growing mountain of books stacked up on the desk and on the floor, I knew Baba meant business, serious business. From what I could make out, his books covered a wide range of subjects, from economics to history. He wanted to know how China had come so far and how we might move ahead. He wanted to learn what had happened to other countries in their early development. And he wanted to understand why our crops had failed.

In the days that followed, I would often wake up late at night to find Baba absorbed in his reading—a cigarette burning in his fingers and the green table lamp casting his large shadow on the wall.

姥姥和姥爺

Lao Lao and Lao Ye

ROM THE TIME I WAS A SMALL CHILD, I WAS AT-
TACHED TO LAO LAO. I LOVED HER DARK AND
SHINY HAIR, HER FAIR, SMOOTH SKIN, AND THE
dimples on her cheeks that deepened as she smiled. And she
smelled like the jasmine flowers in our garden.

Lao Lao was in her mid-forties when I came into her life.
Mama had been assigned to teach at a high school far away and
could not come home during the week to take care of me. Baba
was a screenwriter for an army movie studio, and he, too, had to
travel frequently for his job. Lao Lao became my surrogate
mother. As soon as I was able to walk, I turned into her shadow,
following her everywhere.

As I grew a little older, I began to notice the difference between my grandma and my friends' grandmas. My *lao lao* was
taller than all of them—most other *lao laos* were at least a head
shorter than she. My *lao lao* could read and write, and she often
helped me with my homework, even though, sometimes, I could

Lao Lao, Lao Ye, and me, 1954

not recognize the Chinese characters she wrote—they were of the old, classical kind, whereas the ones I had been studying were simplified. Most other grandmas could barely read. In our courtyard, some of them came to Lao Lao with their correspondence. She would help them write to relatives and read the letters that came back.

But the most noticeable difference between my grandma and other grandmas was that she did not have bound feet. Almost all my neighbors' grandmas walked around our courtyard slowly, as if the dirt under their feet was hurting them. And they never played catch with me. My friend Ming's grandma was Lao Lao's age, but she never joined our games. Once, Di Di and I held on to her hands, trying to force her to play hide-and-seek with us, but Lao Lao asked us to stop.

Curious, one day I asked Lao Lao why she could run with

me but Ming's grandma couldn't, and why she could read and write but the others could not. "I had a good *baba*," she said.

Lao Lao's father—my *zu ye*—had been a butler for a Manchu prince in Beijing in the late 1800s. During one of the many riots in the city, a group of bandits found their way into the prince's mansion, looted its treasures, and demanded to see the master of the house. In the midst of the confusion, Zu Ye led his Manchu employer out through the back door and hid him in a friend's house close by until the bandits left.

In gratitude, the Manchu prince granted Zu Ye a small courtyard house and an allowance, which made it possible for him to marry his childhood sweetheart—a local beauty. Soon, his wife gave birth to a daughter—my *lao lao*. Not long afterward, however, Lao Lao's mama came down with pneumonia and died. Heartbroken, Zu Ye hired a wet nurse and spent much of his time doting on his infant daughter.

It was the custom at the time for girls, aged three or four, to have their feet bound—a traditional ideal of beauty and submission, compelling women to walk slowly. The smaller one's feet, the more desirable one would be considered by her future husband. Following this tradition, Zu Ye asked his sister for help.

Lao Lao's auntie was very fond of her, and every time she came to visit, she would bring a large bag filled with gifts for her niece—new hand-sewn dresses, embroidered handkerchiefs, homemade caramel candies, and pears or peaches from her garden. But that day when Lao Lao eagerly opened the gift bag, she found nothing but roll after roll of white linen cloth, and her auntie looked unusually serious. Silently, she filled up a wooden barrel with warm water and asked Lao Lao to soak her feet. Curious, Lao Lao untied her shoelaces and slowly slid her feet into the water. Her auntie washed her feet with a new bar of soap and dried them gently with a thick towel. Then, she steadied Lao Lao on her bed and took out a roll of white linen.

"This will hurt," she said apologetically, "but after a while, the pain will go away."

Looking from her auntie to her *baba*, who stood tensely watching, Lao Lao did not know what to say. Suddenly, Auntie reached out and bent Lao Lao's toes under, one after another, hard, and started to wrap the linen bandage around Lao Lao's tiny foot, each round of cloth tighter than the last.

The pain came so fast and was so sharp that Lao Lao burst into tears. Tearing the cloth loose from her foot and nearly knocking over the wooden barrel, she ran out of the house. And neither her auntie's pleas nor her *baba*'s coaxing could convince her to go back. She hid in a corner of their courtyard, sobbing.

Zu Ye could not bear to watch his daughter suffer, and the short-lived foot-binding experiment ended. As Lao Lao grew older, her natural beauty and her natural feet surprised people equally. Her father accepted this with good humor, dubbing her feet *tianzu* (heavenly feet).

ᔓ

My *zu ye* was a self-taught scholar who took pride in his fine collection of books and musical instruments. The courageous deed of saving his Manchu prince provided him with the time and means to continue his studies, and he wanted his daughter to be educated, too. But it was not popular at the time for girls to attend public schools. Most of the education they acquired was at their mothers' knees—sewing, cooking, and housekeeping. Zu Ye wanted something better for his child. He hired an elderly tutor who, day by day, tried to drill the teachings of the ancients into Lao Lao's mind, using the age-old method of rote memorization.

The tutor had a long white beard, and always wore a *changpao* (traditional gown). He would close his eyes and cross his legs while reciting the classics by heart. Lao Lao recited after him. Although explaining the books' content was not part of the arrangement, at Zu Ye's insistence the elderly scholar did discuss the meaning of the classic *A Daughter's Canon*.

"Abide by the three obediences, carry out the four virtues," he chanted. This meant that at home a woman should obey her father. After marriage, she should obey her husband. If her husband dies, she should obey her son. For two thousand years now, he added, women of all ages had followed the teachings of these classics—the bibles of womanhood.

"Abide by the three obediences . . ." Lao Lao would chant, rocking her slender body to mimic her tutor, trying to commit the teachings of the sages to memory.

On Lao Lao's seventh birthday, Zu Ye called her to his study. He handed her a redwood box with a yellow silk cover. From it, Lao Lao lifted a delicately carved bamboo lute. An education was not complete, Zu Ye explained, without the knowledge of music and musical instruments. From that day forward, he took upon himself the responsibility of coaching his impressionable young daughter in music.

When she was nine, Lao Lao's carefree childhood came to an end; Zu Ye decided to marry again—and chose a plump woman with nicely bound feet. At first, the stepmother left Lao Lao alone most of the time. Then, after she gave birth, one after another, to her own daughters, the stepmother became more and more resentful of Lao Lao's presence. She seemed to be jealous of Lao Lao's closeness to Zu Ye and used every opportunity to criticize her.

"With her large feet and her scholarly stoop," she would say to Zu Ye time and again, "you'll have a hard time finding her a match, even if you start early."

Zu Ye did not want his beloved daughter to miss out on marriage. Soon after Lao Lao's fifteenth birthday, he started looking for a matchmaker.

The stepmother was not entirely wrong. Lao Lao's unusual inheritance—her *tianzu* as well as her ability to read and write—created a challenge for the neighborhood matchmaker. But Lao Lao's auntie came to her rescue, bringing with her an experienced matchmaker.

"Come and bow to Grandma Zhu," her auntie said by way of introduction. Grandma Zhu looked old, Lao Lao thought. Her face was furrowed with deep lines. Her thinning hair was tied up into a small knot at the back of her head, and she wore an oversize dark-blue jacket. Her bound feet, Lao Lao noticed, were even smaller than her auntie's.

Grandma Zhu pulled Lao Lao closer to her and inspected her from head to toe. "A beautiful girl," she said, looking from Lao Lao to Zu Ye. She stopped for a second while glancing at Lao Lao's feet but said nothing. After this brief introduction, Lao Lao was asked to leave the room. "I know a family that might be just right," Grandma Zhu said as Lao Lao closed the door behind her.

∽

Toward the eastern part of Beijing, not too far from Zu Ye's house, lived the family of an upwardly mobile contractor, the Zhang family, specializing in the construction of courtyard houses. This family did not strictly follow traditions either, for they allowed the eldest son—the natural heir to their business— to pursue medicine instead. The family business, in turn, fell on the shoulders of the second son, my future Lao Ye. Whether he had any other career ambitions, nobody asked. All they knew was that, obediently, he had dropped out of school to take over for his ailing father. Indeed, he eventually took over more than this business; he became the de facto head of the entire family— caring for his aging parents, paying tuition for his two sisters, and watching over his younger brother.

For a man of seventeen, both Grandma Zhu and Zu Ye concluded, Lao Ye qualified as an ideal candidate: he seemed to have a steady character and a stable income, too. They never bothered to consider, however, that my future Lao Ye already had a sweetheart, whom he hoped to marry one day.

Grandma Zhu, beaming from ear to ear, brought the heads of the two households under one roof. With a big smile on his face, the proud father presented the shy bride-to-be: a slender girl in a traditional Chinese silk gown. At five feet eight, she was unusually tall. Her features were refined—she had a moon-shaped face, bright eyes, a slightly tilted nose, and small, soft lips, accentuated by a deep blush.

Both men, the father and the father-in-law-to-be, nodded with admiration at this young woman of careful upbringing. The mother-in-law-to-be, however, could not keep her eyes off the girl's *tianzu*.

"But look at . . ." she whispered in her husband's ear.

"Nonsense," retorted the husband, who prided himself on being a man of his time. And the times were changing in the early 1900s. Imperial dynasties had given way to a republic in 1912. With unbound feet, Lao Lao could be a more efficient helper in the house, said the not only enlightened but also practical father-in-law-to-be. And so the match was settled. "They'll have to live with us, though," he added, "until they have earned enough to build their own house."

With the negotiation completed by the elders, Lao Lao married Lao Ye and moved in with this new family—all total strangers to her. Brought up properly by Zu Ye, Lao Lao took to her daily chores with her head down and her mouth shut. After all, this was how things had been done for thousands of years.

Each morning, the new bride would get up with the servants to prepare breakfast for this family of eight. When breakfast was over and dishes washed, it was almost time to make lunch, followed shortly afterward by dinner. Given that her mother-in-law was a vegetarian in the Buddhist tradition, Lao Lao had to go to the market early every morning to search for green vegetables. In contrast, her father-in-law, being the pragmatic man that he was, believed in nothing as much as the nutritious benefits of fresh meat. The rest of the family inherited his standard, creating quite a challenge for my Lao Lao—who by now had become an almost full-time cook. When steaming dishes were set down, however, she was never at the table with them. The daughter-in-law, according to this family's tradition, could eat only after everyone else was done with the meal.

Any spare time Lao Lao had during the day, she spent caring for her young brother-in-law, playing with him and reading to him from the books she had brought from her father's house. Her wise father-in-law was right. They had gained not only a fine daughter-in-law but a capable cook and a dutiful nanny.

Had she cried over her fate? Was she disappointed with her married life? If Lao Lao ever felt any of these emotions, she buried them deep inside her heart.

One thing she discovered, however, was that sometimes her young husband would disappear late in the day without a word. Worried, one night she set out looking for him—only to find him in bed with his former sweetheart. Shocked, Lao Lao fled, sobbing all the way home.

The next morning, as usual, she got up early and went about her daily chores. Her choices were limited. Divorce initiated by the wife was usually not accepted by the court or the family, at least not because of infidelity. After all, there were still husbands with several wives, all living together following the time-honored tradition of polygamy. Lao Lao, at least in name, was the only wife. Even though Lao Ye's family used her almost like a servant, they had never physically mistreated her, as happened in some families she knew. Besides, she had become increasingly attached to Lao Ye's younger sisters and brother, who looked upon her as both a surrogate mother and a sister. Her freedom, she believed, would be gained by having a son—the first heir to the Zhang family, which would make having her own house legitimate. Finally, her prayers were answered, and the first grandson, my *da jiu*, was born to the family.

After this splendid achievement, Lao Lao discussed having their own house with her husband, and Lao Ye, a happy new father, set out immediately to look for a plot to build a courtyard of their own. Having apprenticed with his own father through his teenage years, Lao Ye was already an experienced contractor. Standing six feet tall, with broad shoulders and a well-tanned face, Lao Ye was a man of few words. He carried all that was thrown on his shoulders without flinching or complaining. Often, to inspect a project's progress, he would climb the bamboo scaffoldings, over thirty feet high, without any harness. Like his father and grandfather before him, he thrived on hard and honest work.

Every courtyard was someone's castle, he believed, and he put his heart and mind into each project. For his own castle, he spread a large-scale map of Beijing on his table and, together with Lao Lao, studied all their options.

A symmetrical city, Beijing was centered on its axis by the Forbidden City—the chief imperial residence for the last five hundred years. Claiming themselves the sons of heaven, the emperors built their temples and monuments along the meridian line. Most of their sons, daughters, and senior consorts settled in grand courtyard houses radiating from the center. By convention this area, Lao Ye and Lao Lao knew very well, was still off-limits to most ordinary people. The western part of Beijing, following tradition, had become home to generations of intelligentsia and some laborers, while the south belonged to different groups of the downtrodden. In the east, slightly off center, lived a mixed population of officials, artists, and varieties of professionals.

As the unofficial head of the family, carrying all the daily responsibilities that came with that role, Lao Ye could not be too far away from his parents. But they should not be too close, either, insisted Lao Lao, hoping that some distance might keep her mother-in-law, with her nicely bound feet, from waggling over to supervise the running of this new household. An appropriate location was finally chosen, not far from Lao Ye's office on the eastern side of town.

On this chosen *hutong* lived a mixed population of retired senior officials in their grand triple courtyards as well as, at a safe distance, some blue-collar workers in their simple shacks

with shared yards. Right in the middle were white-collar workers of all ranks and professions, aspiring to catch up with their
wealthy neighbors through hard work and a bit of luck. Within
this group, Lao Ye and Lao Lao settled on a piece of land that
was originally used as a horse stable for wealthy officials. With
his own construction team, Lao Ye set out to build a courtyard
house of their own.

With the blessing of a feng shui master, hired to make sure
their house would be in harmony with the natural forces, Lao
Ye poured the foundation. Like all the temples, the house sat
squarely in the north of their property and faced south—with
maximum exposure to the sun. Before long, solid gray tiles were
laid seamlessly on the roof. The house had an open floor plan,
with half partitions separating the two bedrooms from the living
room. Adjacent to the main house, they built two small side
apartments for Lao Ye's seasonal workers and, later, our growing
family. To the east and west Lao Ye built two wings, and he completed the south with a matching house. At the southeast corner
was our main entrance, with a heavy wooden door. On it, a cou-
plet was carefully etched by a skilled craftsman:

HONESTY PERSISTS THROUGH THE GENERATIONS;

SCHOLARSHIP LASTS FOREVER.

Lao Lao was overjoyed to finally have a home of her own.
During the early to mid-1930s, a time of relative peace and pros-
perity, she gave birth to four of their six children. But the late

1930s and the 1940s once again ushered a time of chaos into her life. Japanese troops marched into the ancient city of Beijing, followed by eight years of bloody battles between the Japanese forces and the combined powers of the Nationalists and the Communists. As soon as the Japanese were driven out, the Nationalists and the Communists turned their guns on each other.

∽

The Lao Ye who was familiar to me when I was a child in the late 1950s looked very different from the black-and-white picture on Mama's desk. In the photo, Lao Ye looked strong. With an unlit cigar between his lips and a calm but commanding look on his face, he appeared to be the unquestionable center of this large family.

But the Lao Ye I knew was half paralyzed. When he sat in his high-backed armchair, he looked almost like his healthy younger self. When he stood up to walk, he had to drag his left foot and clutch his left hand with his right in order to prevent it from shaking visibly. Every morning, Lao Lao helped slide his left arm into his shirt, which he always insisted on buttoning himself with one hand. From time to time, I'd bring his slippers closer to his feet so that he did not have to bend down. He never resisted my help and always rubbed my head fondly.

"What happened to Lao Ye?" I asked Mama one day when both of us were looking at the old family photo.

She sighed and then told me this story. During the war between the Nationalists and the Communists in the 1940s, people were not building houses anymore, and Lao Ye, checking his ledgers each morning, and calculating and recalculating the numbers on his abacus, could not make his accounts add up. With the coming of a long winter, he knew things would get even worse. Reluctantly, Lao Ye let most of his workers go. Then one day an old friend knocked on his door with a fresh idea.

"I've just come back from the Northeast," the friend said. "There, I saw a brand-new enterprise—people pouring water on the ground and freezing it into a large rink. Then they tie blades onto their boots and slide on the ice. This winter sport is catching on like wildfire with youngsters, bringing in money day and night."

"How can this help us?" asked Lao Ye.

"Since the skating rink is outdoors, someone has to set up tents and encircle the rink. And the same people can also sell tickets and keep the profit."

Lao Ye thought this sounded simple enough, even though it was outside his building experience. After all, how hard could building a simple skating rink be compared with building a house? A reasonable man with a reasonable conclusion, Lao Ye set to work.

He chose a spot close to a city gate where land was cheaper, drove a hard bargain, and leased the land for the winter, using his fine reputation as down payment. The rest would be delivered in installments. Then he called his old crew, who responded within a day. Smiling for the first time in many months, Lao Ye watched his new venture take shape.

Freezing water on the ground was easier than he anticipated, thanks to the subzero temperatures. Behind the ticket counter, he installed dozens of wooden boxes as lockers, complete with new padlocks. Then he set up a large tent, lined with wooden benches for his future customers, and purchased a few hundred pairs of skates. His fine reputation was apparently not enough for the skate merchants, so he borrowed funds from friends. Everyone who could afford to offered his help, knowing Lao Ye's word was a reliable contract.

Then one day, a few weeks before the opening, an unexpected guest—the police chief—showed up. The skating rink, he claimed, was in his jurisdiction, and as a result, Lao Ye would have to pay a fee to the police department.

"How could that be true?" Lao Ye asked. "I've checked with several bureaus and was told that this piece of land is free and clear. Rent to the landlord is my only obligation."

Annoyed by Lao Ye's stubbornness, the police chief left, waving his finger. "Don't say that I didn't warn you."

Lao Ye was not deterred. He had gone too far to look back. Advertisements had already appeared in the local newspapers, paid for again with borrowed money, and more temporary workers had been hired to staff the skating rink. If the weather and customers cooperated, in a few weeks, Lao Ye estimated, he could repay all his debt, giving his family and his workers some much-needed relief.

Beijing's weather in winter was as reliable as a trusted friend. For weeks now, there had been no rain or snow, just stark, bitter cold. The ice rink, swept and groomed day and night, looked like solid, translucent glass. Well-wishers had sent in a dozen pots of yellow chrysanthemums and pink winter plum flowers. Firecrackers, hanging down from the tall bamboo poles supporting the gate, added color and a sense of excitement. All was ready for the opening day, if only people would come.

And they did. Before the big clock at the check-in counter struck nine, lines of eager customers had formed in front of the bamboo gate, rubbing their hands and stamping their feet in the cold. Lao Ye smiled. His luck had returned. The hundreds of firecrackers went off with the opening bell, sending shredded red paper and cheerful explosions whirling into the blue sky. The ticket counter was swamped, and the workers could not hand out locker keys fast enough.

Lao Ye and his friend who had suggested the brilliant idea looked out at the happy scene from Lao Ye's temporary office. "Thanks, my old brother," said a grateful Lao Ye. "I couldn't have done it without you."

Throughout the day, people poured in from all over the city. With nightfall, the skating rink was lit up by spotlights and the crowd grew even larger, as office workers, finishing their workday, joined in for some fun. Lao Ye and his friend never left the window, awed as much by the crowd as by their unbelievable good fortune.

But then, as if from nowhere, a group of young men dressed in black jumped the fences. Rushing toward the ticket counter, they clubbed the stunned workers and broke open the lockers.

Some of them hurled rocks into the crowd. A bloody chaos broke out. Screaming and scrambling, the skaters stumbled in all directions. Like a stampede they crashed into one another with their rental skates. The agile ones made a quick retreat over the fences; others dragged themselves toward the gate.

Lao Ye and his friend burst out of his office, trying desperately to take control of the situation. But they were too late. As quickly as they had appeared, the bandits ran off, and so did most of the customers, leaving the injured strewn across the ice. Then, suddenly, a dozen policemen rushed in, batons waving and whistles blowing. As the familiar face of the police chief approached, Lao Ye dispatched his friend to call for ambulances. He had been set up, and he realized it instantly.

"Don't tell me that I didn't warn you," said the chief smugly, handcuffs in hand. "You are responsible for everyone who is injured here." Then he arrested Lao Ye.

When Lao Lao bailed Lao Ye out the next morning, he was a changed man. Overnight, their hopes had vaporized. Soon, lawsuit after lawsuit was filed by customers or those who claimed to be customers, demanding payment for their lost property, real or not. Many insisted that their lockers held mink coats, sable hats, and brand-new leather jackets. Others blamed the riot for their arthritic legs, sore wrists, and back pain. The creditors, joining the crowd, decided that both Lao Ye's reputation and his credit line had expired overnight and they needed full payment immediately. Lao Ye, always believing his word was assurance enough, had no business insurance. He was ruined.

A proud and honest man, he sold everything that was of any value, including the jewelry that had been Lao Lao's dowry and inheritance. Still, that was not enough to pay the heavy debt. Lao Ye toyed with the idea of selling their courtyard house, but Lao Lao would not hear of it. The compromise was that they would keep the principal house on the north side and rent out the others. With creditors and lawyers at his door every day, Lao Ye was forced to borrow more money, even though willing lenders were slow in coming. Then one night in early 1949, at age forty, Lao Ye was seized by a stroke and paralyzed.

The sudden change of fortune hit Lao Lao as hard as it did Lao Ye. Overnight, all her dreams were shattered. Packing her children into the northern house, she now had the added full-time responsibility of caring for her invalid husband, a broken man. How she managed in those days, I could only imagine, for she never talked about it, and I never pried. Some memories, like corpses, are better left buried.

One thing I did learn from others was that Lao Lao was the one who kept the family together. She wrote to their lenders, begging for lenience and payment extensions. She rummaged through all their possessions and bartered anything that was of value. And she made sure her children stayed in school. There was nothing she wouldn't do for her family.

Lao Lao's family included everyone she loved—friends, neighbors, strangers. When her sons brought two orphaned friends home, Lao Lao, without any hesitation, laid extra chop-sticks on the dining table and invited them to stay.

Lao Lao in our courtyard, 1960s

In our courtyard, the wives and mothers of the electrician and the tailor had always benefited from Lao Lao's education. Many people were illiterate in those days, and when, in the early 1950s, the new government tried to recruit those who could lend a hand as volunteer teachers, Lao Lao extended hers. And so, at ten o'clock every morning, the wives came into her home, lugging the government's free books under their arms and bringing their friends. My mama found Lao Lao a small blackboard, which she propped on the dining table for her class. On it Lao Lao wrote, "China, Party. Love China. Love Party," quotations from the government textbooks. Word by word she helped her keen students practice writing on the blackboard, their faces radiant with excitement. For the first time in her life, Lao Lao felt respected. Her education had become an asset at last.

Both Lao Lao's reputation and her class steadily grew. Soon they had to move to a bigger room. Now, in addition to the morning classes, she taught in the afternoon. Her students consulted her not only about the books she taught but about personal matters as well.

Learning had always been equated with wisdom in this country, and Lao Lao was now looked upon as a learned woman—a role she was uncomfortable with at first but soon grew into. As a child, I would tag along with her to our neighbors' houses, where she would bring chicken soup to sick housewives, then sit on the edges of their beds and hold the hands of those who were sobbing and pouring their hearts out to her.

Our neighbors were grateful, and they all began to call her Mama. For several years, they expressed their gratitude by electing Lao Lao to represent the district in the All-China Women's Federation, the largest and most prestigious women's organization in the country. Lao Lao was reborn.

During those happy days in the early 1950s, Lao Lao could never have imagined that thick, dark clouds would once again gather in her life and threaten the safety of this large extended family she loved with all her heart.

暴雨将临

The Gathering Storm

OST PEOPLE CANNOT REMEMBER WHEN THEIR CHILDHOOD ENDED. I, ON THE OTHER HAND, HAVE A CRYSTAL-CLEAR MEMORY OF THAT MO-ment. It happened one night, in the summer of 1966, when my elementary school headmaster hanged himself. I was twelve years old.

Three years earlier, I had been among some one hundred children selected to attend the Foreign Language School. Our country needed to step up its language training, Baba explained to me excitedly, now that China had resumed diplomatic ties with several European powers. That year, in Beijing alone, two boarding schools, including mine, were set up to teach students as young as nine to speak several languages. The expectation was that, after ten years of training, many of the students would continue their studies in leading universities, with the possibility of diplomatic careers waiting for them when they graduated.

In the summer of 1963, I was busy getting ready for this

Mama, Di Di, Baba, and me, 1963

new chapter in my life. The language school, located outside the city gate, was a good two-hour bus ride from home. All students were to live on campus during the week. While waiting for school to start, I spent most of my days saying goodbye to my former schoolmates and watching grownups prepare me for my new journey. In my closet was a growing collection of new possessions—a light blue quilt and matching pillows with little yellow flowers, carefully sewn by Lao Lao; a porcelain washbasin with pink peonies painted on it; two pairs of blue pants and two white blouses; colorful new notebooks and pencils, gifts from my classmates; a little pink folding mirror, a gift from Yi Yi, my youngest Auntie; and a green denim school bag, a gift from my parents. Baba had once talked about what it was like for him leaving home at fifteen to join the army in 1945 at the end of the War of Resistance. I felt, at this moment, a strange connection with his experience, at least with the leaving home part of it, as I wondered what boarding school life would be like.

On the western outskirts of Beijing, where the city bus stopped and the commuter bus began, was a sprawling piece of farmland. Dotted along the unpaved road were clusters of old graves covered with wild grass. An old workers' and farmers' civil service training school was hidden behind a few rows of mud village houses. A few years before, it had been turned into a language school for high school students. Now an elementary school and a middle school had been added.

When I joined over a hundred other nine-year-olds on registration day, the school looked festive. Colorful flags lined the entrance and the roadsides, and a giant red banner, with HUAN-YING (WELCOME) pasted on it, hung across the iron gate. Many high school students were waiting at the doorway to help with our luggage. I waved goodbye to Lao Lao and Mama at the gate and smiled shyly at my high school guide—a tall girl with long braids.

"Call me Lan," she said as she reached out her hand and clasped mine before bending down to pick up my bag. In a daze, I walked with her along the road paved with jagged cement tiles, heading toward my dormitory. We passed row after row of one-story gray brick classrooms, with window frames and doors newly painted in dark green. I stopped by the one with a white wooden sign attached to the edge of its door—CLASS NO. 2—my classroom. I pushed the door open and stepped inside. In front of me was a familiar setup—wooden desks, with tops that flipped open, were lined up side by side, six in a column. A teacher's podium stood before a brand-new blackboard. On it, drawn with red chalk, were once again the two large characters for *Huanying*. A portrait of Chairman Mao, unframed, was pinned above the blackboard. I sat down at a desk in the front row, adjusted my seat slightly, and tried to imagine what it would be like to be in this class.

Later, as my tour continued, Lan pointed out our kitchen and cafeteria. I stuck my head into the kitchen and saw an old cook with a large iron ladle, stirring up something in a huge wok. Behind the cafeteria was an empty hall. All of our school assemblies were held there, Lan told me.

Next to the assembly hall was an orchard. "Look at the red apples on those trees," Lan said, her face lighting up. She picked one up from the ground and showed it to me. The branches were bent low by the weight of these big apples. I stood on my toes and touched one with my fingertips.

Then we crossed the orchard and circled the soccer field and running track. Finally, we arrived at my three-story dormitory, shaded by a row of tall poplar trees. Leading me into a room on the top floor, Lan smiled. "Choose any bed you like," she said. "You are lucky to be the first."

There were four bunk beds in the bedroom and two small desks. I sat down on a bed next to the window, and Lan put my luggage on top of it. "Enjoy," she said, swinging her long braids back, "and let me know if you need anything else."

After she left, I unpacked my new possessions. Looking at

them scattered on my wooden bed, I suddenly felt homesick. The reality of having to spend six days a week with total strangers hit me. I missed Lao Lao, I missed Di Di, and I missed our little courtyard.

As I sat on the edge of my bed, trying to hold back tears, a girl bounced into the room. "This is *my* room, too," she said, pointing at the number on our door. "My name is Wen," she added, extending her hand. Before I could reply, she whirled around in her bright red skirt and parked herself right next to me. "We'll be friends," she said, her hand on my lap. "I just know it!"

Wen's warmth and confidence eased, at least for the moment, my feeling of sadness. "What a beautiful mirror," she said, picking up my pink mirror, unfolding it, and standing it on the desk. "Let's go and see what's going on outside." She reached over to hold my hand in hers, and we ran out together. I had a friend.

At the crack of dawn the following morning, we gathered for our first school assembly. Our headmaster, who was in charge of both the elementary and high schools, addressed us from the podium. A short, gray-haired man with heavy glasses, he spoke slowly with a slight southern accent.

"Welcome," he said in a calm, gentle voice. "From now on, this school is your home."

I liked his soft voice and ready smile. That day, he talked about our mission and the high expectations bestowed upon us by the country and the Party. Next to him stood our deputy headmaster, a lanky man who was in charge of our new elementary school. The day before, he had welcomed us at our dorm with his little daughter skipping along by his side, her two pigtails woven together with red ribbons. He had sat down on my bed with his daughter on his lap.

"Are you homesick?" he asked, his eyes smiling, as his fingers stroked his daughter's hair. I lowered my head, too shy to answer.

"Come and visit us anytime," he said, patting me gently on the shoulder. "We live just on the other side of campus." His little girl nodded to me, her dimples deepening as she smiled.

∽

Boarding school life, as I soon found out, was very structured. At six o'clock, we woke up to the blaring school bell, rubbed our eyes, and jumped out of bed for morning exercise. Led by our teachers, who boarded at the school with us, we stretched, marched in formation, and jogged around the track. Here, day was still part of night, with stars shining in the predawn sky. By the end of the morning drill, when we could just glimpse the rising sun, we were wide-awake.

After a quick washup, we assembled in the cafeteria, where tables were already arranged for groups of ten. A warm and welcoming smell of steamed buns and rice porridge filled the room. Each one of us took a turn helping the chefs by coming early to set up the tables and cleaning up afterward. Not a drop should be left in the rice bowl or on the table, we were reminded constantly—"Just think about the starving children in Africa." I did try to imagine them, with large, hungry eyes, bony little arms, and skinny hands holding out big, empty bowls, begging by the roadside. I'd seen them this way in many newspaper photos. Sometimes the student on duty would point out tiny bits of leftovers from certain tables, and that was enough to fill us with guilt.

English class was my favorite, taught by Teacher Chen and a white-haired woman from London, Miss Cohen. "English phonetics are very much like your phonetic system," Miss Cohen liked to say in her high-pitched voice, "and the easiest way to learn is to sing along." That day we learned our first English song, "A, B, C." From there we progressed to "London Bridge Is Falling Down," and "I'm a Little Teapot."

Teacher Chen looked like my mother's twin sister— straight-backed, with shiny black hair and big, expressive eyes. Also, like my mother, she had a gentle intensity about her. When the gentleness faded into intensity, I knew I had better watch out.

One day, she brought twelve little mirrors to class and distributed them among us. "The English *o* is pronounced differently from a Chinese *o*," she explained. "To make an English *o*, you must learn to push the vowel sound from the front of your mouth to the far back. Look into the mirror and see if you can tell the difference." In between making faces in the mirror and at one another, we passed our first *o* test.

An accomplished amateur actress, Teacher Chen wrote plays for us to perform in English. For *Little Red Riding Hood,* she brought all of the props to class, complete with a red velvet cape, a handmade face mask painted in black ink for the big, bad wolf, and little reading glasses and a fluffy nightcap for the old grandma. We quickly memorized every line and took turns acting the play out in front of the classroom. Our teachers made learning fun.

But no matter how much fun my classes were, I often felt homesick, particularly in the afternoon, when I had some time to roam around on my own. I shed more than a few tears in secret. Sometimes, I would beg our school's old gatekeeper to let me use his phone to call home. As soon as Lao Lao picked up the receiver, I would burst into tears. Afraid that the gatekeeper would not want to lend his phone to a crybaby again, I would try hard to hold back my sobbing. Lao Lao's voice also sounded shaky on the other end of the line. She would ask me what I'd like to eat when I came home on the weekend and would promise me that she would be the first one waiting at the school gate on Saturday afternoon to pick me up.

Within a few weeks, however, playtime became more structured, leaving little opportunity for secret tears or phone calls home. Various extracurricular groups were formed to teach us Ping-Pong, dance, drawing, track and field, and even how to raise rabbits and silkworms. I was not much of a dancer, nor was I a fast runner. So I settled on the rabbits, remembering how fond I had been of those Lao Lao raised. My new friend Wen signed on with me.

Close to the rabbit pen was the school's stable, home to two horses, a donkey, and an amiable old man—Uncle Wang, as we came to call him. Uncle Wang tended to the animals night and day, and used them to transport vegetables and firewood for our school kitchen. Living alone, Uncle Wang was a veteran handyman. He was a favorite among the students, who were attracted by his animated stories, his saintly patience, and his farm animals. He was also in charge of my rabbit team—a job he attended to with encyclopedic knowledge and childlike enthusiasm. Whenever we had free time after class, we would gather in his room, begging for more stories. During one of these visits, we noticed that one of the horses' bellies was growing bigger.

"Is she going to have a baby soon?" I asked.

"In a few weeks," Uncle Wang announced, beaming.

"Could we watch the delivery?"

Uncle Wang said that we could. None of us had ever witnessed a birth, let alone the birth of a baby horse.

"Will it be a boy or a girl?" Wen asked.

"Wait and see," Uncle Wang said with a smile.

We waited and waited. When the day finally arrived, Uncle Wang moved the mother-to-be into the stable yard, now encircled by a temporary wooden fence and cushioned with soft grass from the farm, with the fresh scent of the field still in it. Like anxious relatives, we ran to visit her every time we could, including our ten-minute breaks between classes. The mother-to-be, by contrast, appeared to be patient and resigned, even though her slender body was distorted, weighed down by a new life.

At last, right after dinner, when four of us made our way to

the stable for the tenth time that day, we found the mare silhou-
etted against the gentle glow of the setting sun, with Uncle
Wang and the school doctor turned veterinarian on either side.
The new life was there; we could sense it struggling already to be
freed. Would it be healthy? Would it be strong?

"There is nothing more common than birth," Uncle Wang
said. "Millions are born into the world as we speak and millions
die, but nothing is more magical and mysterious than witnessing
the birth of a new life, a new creation."

Suddenly, the mare crouched down. Her heavy breathing
turned into deep and agonized groans. Uncle Wang and the
doctor were on their knees, too, as if begging the pain to stop
and life to begin, sweat pouring down their foreheads in the
mid-autumn night. Any minute now, I thought, as my heart began to race and I started to breathe heavily, too.

Hours seemed to have passed, with emotions—anxiety, expectation, and fear—ebbing and flowing through us like waves.
We completely forgot about study hall. Before the last purple
cloud disappeared into the oncoming darkness, the mare kicked
and moaned again. The doctor and Uncle Wang were now on all
fours, trying to coax the foal into this world. The mother trembled, and then we saw two tiny hooves, then the front legs, then
a nose, wet and soft, then the head, and at last the whole foal
slide out of the mare and into the waiting arms of the doctor.

There was no sound—either from the mare or from us. It
seemed any sound would disturb a waking dream. With the
help of Uncle Wang, the doctor tied the umbilical cord and

cut it, separating, for the first time and forever, the new life from the old. The baby's nostrils twisted gently as she took in her first breath on earth. The mare trembled again and then relaxed on the soft grass, turning her head toward the sky, as if to watch the last trail of purple clouds disappear beyond the horizon.

Finally we found our voices. We screamed with joy and hugged one another.

"Would you accept the privilege of naming the newborn?" asked Uncle Wang. We looked at one another in disbelief. "Come back tomorrow with some ideas," he said. "Now, hurry on to study hall."

Flushed with excitement, we decided to come up with two choices each. Walking back to our dorm slowly after class, we shared our ideas one after another.

"Purple Cloud," exclaimed Wen, remembering the brief yet decisive moment when the filly was born. From that day, we adopted Purple Cloud, bringing her fresh grass from nearby farms and helping to clean the stable any chance we got.

Returning from home the following Sunday, Wen danced into our bedroom, waving a piece of shimmering purple silk. "Let's make a banner for Purple Cloud," she said. With great care, we sewed the filly's name on the banner with yellow thread, and Uncle Wang proudly pinned it on the stable wall.

The semester moved on. Quite often in the late afternoon, our teachers would take us to a nearby park with a pond teaming with tadpoles and shining little fish. Plastic bags in hand, we would scoop up tadpoles with our hands, place them in the bags, and walk gingerly back to our dorm. There, we would transfer our prey into a bigger porcelain basin and try to raise them. I do not remember seeing any of them reach maturity, but that was certainly not for lack of care. Gradually, my feelings about being away at school were changing, until one day I was homesick no more.

ᔕᓬ

Three years passed quickly at the Foreign Language School, where I studied hard, made friends, and had fun. Then, when I was twelve, everything changed.

In the late spring of 1966, we began to hear about disturbances at Beijing and Tsinghua Universities, two leading institutions of higher learning. *Dazibao* (large-character posters) had appeared on their campuses, accusing the school authorities of departing from Chairman Mao's teachings. The posters demanded that colleges open their doors to workers and peasants instead of the privileged minority. Classes were suspended and students began to form spontaneous groups, calling themselves Red Guards, words they proudly displayed on their red armbands.

Then, one day in midsummer, Chairman Mao himself stood on top of the Gate of Heavenly Peace, where seventeen years before he had proclaimed, in his deep voice thick with a Hunan accent, the founding of the People's Republic of China. This time, clad in a green army uniform, he waved to a million adoring young faces—Red Guards gathered at Tiananmen Square, eager for a view of the Chairman.

"I support our brave Red Guards," he announced to the world, accepting a red armband presented to him by a student leader, thereby giving his official approval to the movement. Like wildfire catching a favorable wind, Red Guard units appeared in every university and high school, and posters denouncing school authorities were displayed on every campus.

Our elementary school was quiet, like the stillness before a storm. Separated from the high school by rows of gray buildings, we were instructed to carry on with our daily routine, while the other side of the campus was simmering with excitement. Many of the high school students formed Red Guard units of their own. Like soldiers in the army, they dressed up in green uniforms, with brown leather belts around their waists. On their left arms, they wore strips of red cloth with bright yellow characters spelling out *hongweibing* (Red Guard) on them.

From time to time, I could hear them rehearsing the now popular song—

Use our pens as weapons,
Aim at the dark force,
Together—teachers and students—rise in rebellion,
To become pathbreakers of the Cultural Revolution.

Extol Chairman Mao and our Party,
The Party is our real mother and father,
Whoever dares to challenge our Party,
We will immediately send him to hell—
Kill, kill, kill.

One afternoon, overtaken by curiosity, several of us decided to sneak out during rest period and visit our high school friends. On the way, we discovered a small crowd buzzing in front of our headmaster's office. Shoving my way through, I saw a Red Guard standing on a short ladder, pasting a notice on the wall. It was Lan—my old guide—dressed in an oversize army uniform, with both sleeves rolled up. On her left arm, fastened to her sleeve with a large steel safety pin, was a brand-new red armband. Her thick, waist-long braids had been chopped into two short ponytails that barely touched her shoulders.

Before this time of unrest, Lan had occasionally come to visit me in my dorm like an adopted older sister. Lately, I had not seen her, but I had heard she had become a leader of the Red Guards. Today, she looked like someone I hardly knew. Her sisterly warmth had disappeared. Instead I saw only anger. She looked right at us but didn't appear to even recognize me. Then she turned back to smooth the edges of the poster, still dripping with black ink.

LI PING, CONFESS YOUR CRIME! shouted the headline. YOU POISON OUR MINDS WITH WESTERN IDEOLOGY, AND YOU TRAIN STUDENTS TO FOLLOW CAPITALISM INSTEAD OF COMMUNISM.

I was in shock. Li Ping was our headmaster. How could he, a man with such a gentle smile and scholarly, thick glasses, try to poison us? I asked myself. Turning toward my friends, I saw the same stunned look on their faces.

"Let's go find my sister," Wen suggested. "She'll know what's happened." Wen's oldest sister, Ling, was the president of her senior class—someone, Wen and I believed, who was destined for greatness.

We found Ling sitting alone at the back of her classroom. With dark circles under her eyes, she looked like she hadn't slept for days. I glanced at her arm—there was no red armband.

"What happened?" Wen asked.

"I don't know," she said. "Lots of people were on the attack list, including me. They said I was a follower of the headmaster and would not let me join the Red Guards."

"We saw Lan pasting a poster on the wall accusing the headmaster," I stuttered, knowing that Lan and Ling were friends.

A sad smile crossed Ling's face. "She wouldn't talk to me after my name appeared on the accused list." Then, Ling turned to her little sister with upsetting news. "Dad has been taken away. He's still not back."

Before Wen could ask any more questions, Ling's tone of voice became more positive. "Chairman Mao supports the Red Guards," she said. "So we should have faith." As we left Ling, we felt even more confused than before.

∽

Every day added more uncertainty to life on campus. Now there were posters everywhere—on the walls of the auditorium, the dormitories, and all the administrative buildings. Some posters had even spread to our elementary school. The list of the accused included not only the headmasters but also some of our teachers. Our math teacher, an amiable man in his sixties, was singled out as a "filthy traitor" because he had allegedly coached the son of a Japanese general in math during World War II. Teacher Chen, my favorite English teacher, was barred from the classroom after being accused of polluting young minds with Western fairy tales and mythology. Worried, I went to knock on her bedroom door several times; no one answered.

Miss Cohen had also left us, unannounced. When one class after another was canceled, I found myself with unexpected free time each day. Not knowing what to do, Wen and I roamed aimlessly around campus, running toward crowds wherever they gathered.

Waking up early one morning from a troubled sleep, I stumbled out of the dormitory for some fresh air. Immediately I saw several Red Guards from our high school rushing toward the administrative building. Curious, I ran after them. Even from a distance, I could hear yelling and screaming coming toward me like waves from the sea. A crowd had gathered in front of the headmaster's office. Fighting my way through it, I found our headmaster, his thick glasses smashed on the ground and his head and nose bleeding. A tall Red Guard pushed him up against the brick wall.

"Confess," screamed the student at the top of his lungs.

"Confess, confess!" his comrades chimed in.

"But I have done nothing wrong." The headmaster gasped for breath. "I've always been loyal to the Party."

"Liar!" Grabbing the headmaster by the collar, the tall Red Guard raised his fist.

I started trembling; then I turned and pushed my way out of the crowd. Running as fast as I could back to my room, I collapsed on my bed.

"What happened?" asked Wen and my other roommates, still rubbing their sleepy eyes.

"They are beating the headmaster," I whispered.

"What?" They all bolted out of bed.

"Don't go," I pleaded. "Please don't go!"

As if not hearing what I had just said, they quickly dressed and dashed out. Pretty soon, Wen staggered back into the room, her eyes wide with disbelief. After that, I stopped running toward any crowd.

Later, I asked Wen if she had news about her father. "He's back," she said, tears welling up. "But he is covered with bruises."

"What are you going to do?"

Wiping away her tears, Wen announced, "I'm going home. There's a storage room hidden in the back of our yard. My sisters have asked my father to hide there whenever someone knocks on our door. If they dare to take him away again, we'll fight them."

Several of our classmates had already left for home; one more disappearance at school would not be noticed. "I'll come visit you soon," I assured her.

Classes became even more sporadic, and teachers were too preoccupied with their own troubles to pay us much attention. Our disciplined life of the previous three years felt more and more like a distant memory.

Then one morning, not long after Wen had left for home, I

came out of our dorm to find several of my classmates huddled at the door, their faces tense with fear.

"What's wrong?" I asked.

"They say our headmaster has killed himself," one of them answered. "They say he's hanged himself on a big tree at Fragrant Hill."

"They found a note in his pocket, saying that he's loyal to the Party and to Chairman Mao," another one added.

I froze, numb, haunted again by the recent memory of seeing him pushed against the wall, his shattered glasses tossed in the dirt. That night, I had a hard time falling asleep. When I finally did, I had a vivid dream. I could see our headmaster dangling from a thick branch, a rope tightened around his neck. His broken glasses, taped together with strips of bandages, hung loosely from one ear, and one of his shoes had fallen to the ground.

Now I retreated to my room as much as I could. It was the one place on campus where I felt safe from the chaos, until one afternoon a Red Guard came to our dorm, a loudspeaker in hand.

"Everyone, out!" she yelled. "You must come join our condemnation meeting in the assembly hall."

I reluctantly followed my classmates and inched my way to the far corner of the hall. Our deputy headmaster was being pushed onto the stage by several high school Red Guards. His cheeks were ashen, and his hair had turned gray. Kicking him behind the knees, a Red Guard forced him to kneel.

Suddenly, another Red Guard pushed her way toward the

podium, holding the hand of the deputy headmaster's daughter. It was Lan.

"Denounce your father," she ordered. "Denounce him with this stick."

Confused and scared, the seven-year-old started to cry.

"Chairman Mao's children never shed tears," Lan said, raising her voice. "You said you love Chairman Mao, right?"

The girl nodded, sobbing.

"Then you must denounce your father."

With Lan's fingers clutching her own, the young girl, still choked with tears, raised her hand. I tried to cover my eyes, but I watched the stick come down on her father's head—and tears roll down his cheeks.

I packed up my bag that afternoon and hurried out of the school gate. I was determined not to set foot there ever again. Never before had I pined so much for the peaceful refuge of our little courtyard.

无家可归

Home No More

ONCE, AS A CHILD, I WAS CAUGHT IN A RAIN-STORM WHILE PLAYING IN A PARK. SUDDENLY, THE SKY DARKENED AND THE WIND SWEPT everything—dirt, loose tree branches, scraps of paper—off the ground. Thunder crashed while lightning flashed in the distance. Luckily there was a pavilion nearby, and I ran toward it. With its sloping roof, the old pavilion sheltered me, even though its sides were wide open. There, on this little island of refuge, I watched and waited for the weather to clear. But soon, sheets of cold rain slashed right through the pavilion, soaking me to the bone. I realized there was no safety here—the storm had engulfed everything.

Like that storm, the deluge of Red Guard violence at the language school swept over me with such unexpected force that there was little I could do but flee. Moving back to the sanctuary of our courtyard home, though reassuring, was also strange. It had been three years since I had started boarding school. Now, as always, Lao Lao's hugs made me feel safe. Even the smell of ginger and pepper in her kitchen was comforting. But I missed my school friends and worried about what was going to happen to some of my favorite teachers. Were they going to be beaten like our headmasters?

I feared for Mama, too. She had been transferred to Beijing's Red Sun Middle School as dean of students. Before this, she had taught for years at a country school far away. I remember missing her when I was little. Every Saturday morning, Di Di and I would carry our little stools outside, sit in front of our gate, and wait for her to appear. As soon as we spotted her from the far end of our *hutong*, we would run as fast as we could to meet her. Then she would bend down and gather us both in her arms. Now, for the first time that I could remember, she would be home during the week and I could have dinner with her every night. But I soon discovered she was often too tired to talk and seemed preoccupied, as if she was hiding something from me.

No longer a deep sleeper as I once had been, I woke up early one morning from a bad dream. Everyone else was still sound asleep. Quietly, I pushed open our wooden gate and stepped out into the misty dawn to see if I could catch a peddler and buy some fried dough for an early breakfast. There, a big poster snapped me awake. In bold characters, it accused Lao Lao of being an enemy of the people and the wife of a filthy capitalist. Lao Lao! My Lao Lao, who had helped so many people! Lao Ye was not even alive anymore—he had passed away years before—but that did not seem to matter. Anger rose inside me, and I ran to wake up Di Di to show him what I had seen.

"I have an idea," he said, then disappeared. A minute later Di Di returned, a penknife in hand. Holding him up with both arms, I kept an eye on the street while he hacked at the poster, slashing it with all his strength until it was in shreds. Then, throwing the knife onto the ground, he tore down what was left of the poster.

We snuck back into our courtyard and threw the shredded poster into the toilet. Satisfied, we crawled into bed.

A few hours later, noise from the yard woke me with a start. Someone was yelling at Lao Lao. "What have you done to the poster? How dare you destroy it!" I peeked through the curtain and recognized the teenage son and daughter of a neighbor. The brother, red with rage, was hollering at Lao Lao. I pulled my quilt up over my head and began to cry. "Please, please," I begged in my heart, "don't hurt Lao Lao."

Suddenly, there was commotion outside our courtyard. Distracted, the brother and sister turned to leave.

"We'll be watching you," they shouted at Lao Lao on their way out.

Soon after this incident, I learned what was bothering Mama. Like my old headmaster from the language school, she had been accused of abandoning Chairman Mao's teaching and poisoning the students' minds. Now, night after night, I would find her sitting at the desk writing "confessions" of her alleged offense, demanded by the Red Guards at her school. Then, one day, she told us she had been ordered to board at school with the rest of the senior administrators.

That morning, Di Di and I helped carry her bags to the school. There, a classroom had been turned into a temporary bedroom. Several beat-up bunk beds sat in the corners. The headmistress was already in the room, trying to cover her hard wooden bunk with some worn blankets. She was wearing a faded blue jacket, and her white hair kept falling over her face when she bent down to straighten her bed. She turned and gave us a sad, silent nod as we entered.

Di Di and I stretched Mama's green quilt on another bed. It was the same cover she had used years ago when she was in the army—fighting for a new China. Mama had refused to throw it away, and Lao Lao had patched the holes in it with different fabrics. Now the quilt looked like an old map of the world.

Through the open window, Mama suddenly spotted a group of Red Guards striding toward us. She turned to Di Di and me, insisting that we leave immediately. Reluctantly, we dragged ourselves out of the room, looking back at her every few steps. She was still standing at the window motionless as we turned the corner into the busy street.

The next day, Di Di and I went to see her again, bringing dumplings from Lao Lao. On our way back home, two of Mama's students followed us. I looked at Di Di, and we doubled our speed. The students kept pace with us. When we turned the corner into a quiet alley, they suddenly began to hurl rocks at us.

"Don't visit her anymore," one of them howled. "She is our enemy!"

Di Di picked up a stone, ready to fight back, but I grabbed his hand and started to run, knowing that at eleven and twelve we were no match for the older students. They came after us until our neighbor Uncle Liu happened by on his way home from work. He stopped them with a loud curse and a raised fist.

Taken by surprise, the students sneered at us. "We'll be back. And we know where you live," they bellowed before finally turning and running down the *hutong*.

Suddenly I no longer felt safe anywhere—not even at home.

∽

After our encounter with Mama's students, Lao Lao and Baba decided that Di Di and I should move with our *baba* to his movie studio, for the military had not yet been swept up into the political upheaval. I asked Lao Lao to come with us, since she would be home alone and the neighborhood Red Guards still had their eyes on her. But Lao Lao shook her head.

"I have to take care of our houses," she said. "And your mama, aunties, and uncles will need me when they come back. Go with Baba," she added. "I'll come to see you soon." And so, reluctantly, Di Di and I followed Baba out the door.

Baba's movie studio was about two hours by bus from our house. It reminded me of my language school—with rooming houses spread out in the middle of open farmland. A lake, surrounded by weeping willows and a few makeshift wooden benches, lay on one side of the spacious compound. A few old farmers squatted by the lakeside during the day, fishing poles in hand.

Since its inception in the early 1950s, the studio, funded by the military, had been dedicated primarily to making feature films and documentaries about the history of the army and the heroic lives of the soldiers. Some eight hundred families called this large compound home—providing a ready supply of possible playmates. Used to campus life by now, I made friends quickly.

At the studio, most grownups were called day and night to meetings where they were briefed on events happening around the country and where they studied the latest instructions from Mao and the Party. That left us children to fend for ourselves— free to do as we pleased. Di Di and I spent much of our time with two new friends—Yun, a girl my age, and her brother, Lin, who was a few years older. We bought food coupons from the canteen and carried them in our pockets so that whenever our stomachs growled, we just ran to the canteen, tore a page out of the coupon book, took whatever was available from the food stand, gobbled it down, and dashed out again. To us, eating seemed a necessary nuisance. The days were too short, and we had plenty to do.

Early on, we spent much of our time playing by the lake. Lin had accompanied his father to the lake countless times and had mastered the art of fishing. Putting on his father's big straw hat, he would start his routine early in the morning, with a fishing pole in one hand and a rusty bucket in the other. He followed the narrow dirt road that separated the lake from the cornfield in search of earthworms. Before I knew it, he had gathered enough worms to fill the bottom of his bucket. Then he surveyed the lake, found a strategic location under a big willow tree, and put his bait onto the hook. Pulling the edge of his straw hat down farther, he would squat there patiently for the whole morning. Yun and I would sometimes go with him, but neither of us had the patience to last very long before we were distracted by other activities, such as catching dragonflies with Di Di.

My brother had become a skillful dragonfly catcher. With a homemade net tied to a bamboo pole, he would hide behind a tall tree, like a hunter waiting for his prey, then spring out when a dragonfly landed. The best time to catch them, he said, was just before a rainstorm, for then the dragonflies circled low. I tried to imitate him but had no luck.

Then, with Yun, I discovered the studio's outdoor swimming pool. Heated naturally by the sun, the water felt heavenly. My days at the movie studio were full of easy pleasures. In this happy oasis, I began to feel as if life might become normal again.

∽

The beginning of our school year in September came and went. I had no homework, nor had I read a single book for months. Surprisingly, I began to feel bored—as if I was living in a time warp, with the same weary images repeating themselves over and over. "What's going to happen to us?" I asked Yun.

But before I could find my bearings, the political upheaval at Baba's studio, like the looming storm I had experienced in the old pavilion, became more and more inevitable, until one day it finally swept in, exposing me once again to the fury of the elements.

Living next door to our temporary apartment was a gentle young couple. The husband was a well-known composer; the wife—Aunt Song, as I came to call her—had once been an actress. Childless, they treated my brother and me as their surrogate children.

Aunt Song treasured her soft, shining hair, which, when let loose, cascaded down her shoulders like black silk. I admired it, too, combing and braiding it for her often. After the start of the Cultural Revolution, long hair, like expensive clothing and accessories, was deemed unfit for the movement's puritanical ideals. A simple army uniform, provided you were lucky enough to get one, and short, straight hair became the new fashion. Soon, short hair came to be more than just a standard; it turned into a requirement. With no hesitation or regret, I cut my own long braids into shoulder-length ponytails. As a young teenager, I was happy to follow the latest fashions.

To Aunt Song, however, cutting her hair was like parting with an old friend. Every day, she rolled it up into a big bun and hid it under an oversize army cap, only letting it down in the presence of a few people, including me. She would comb it gently each morning with an ivory comb before putting it up in a voluminous pile behind her head. Sometimes I would try to fasten the bun for her with large steel hairpins.

Early one morning I waved to her from the balcony as she walked to the farmers' market outside the studio, a bamboo basket in hand. Not even ten minutes had passed before I heard a loud knock on the door. It was Aunt Song, with scissors in her shaking hands.

At first, she could not even speak. I brought her a glass of water and sat her down. Finally, she explained. "There are Red Guards at the gate with rusty scissors, trying to cut anyone's hair that's not short enough." She looked at me, and then put the scissors she'd been holding into my hands. "Cut it for me."

"Me?" I was stunned by the request. "I'm not good at cutting hair."

"Better you do it than them." She sighed. "At least you will be gentle."

I looked down at the scissors.

"Come," she said, sitting down in front of my mirror. "It's all right."

Feeling her soft, black hair, loose on her shoulders for the last time, my hands started to tremble. It had only taken two easy snips when I cut off my own braids, but now my first two attempts didn't even make a dent. Finally, I bit my lip, steadied my hand, and took a deep breath; waves of black, silky hair fell down her shoulders to the floor.

"Now it's my turn," I found myself saying. "Come and cut my hair, too." I did not quite understand why I said this, whether to comfort her or to show camaraderie. "I have always wanted my hair shorter anyway."

"Are you sure?" she asked.

"Yes. Do it!"

Pulling out the ivory comb from her pocket, she sat me down at the mirror. Layer by layer, she lifted my hair gently and with an expert hand cut it, stepping back from time to time to look at her creation.

"I should have had you cut it a long time ago," I said. Then, crawling across the floor on my hands and knees, I picked up each lock of her long, loose hair, now mixed with mine, and carefully put them in a plastic bag. "Our souvenirs," I told her.

∽

The peaceful shelter we had found at Baba's movie studio was beginning to crack open. In the days that followed, it shattered completely. Early one morning, a few days after I had butchered Aunt Song's hair, I heard a knock on my window and saw Yun's anxious face through the glass. I sensed it was not a call to go fishing—something was wrong. Scrambling out of bed, I let her into the room.

"They took my dad away this morning," she said in a hushed voice, "and ordered us to move from the compound."

Yun's father, Uncle Chen, was the head of the movie studio, and their family of four lived in a sunny three-bedroom apartment next to our building.

"Where will you go?" I asked.

"Into a shack outside the compound." She lowered her head with tears in her eyes.

I hurried with Yun to see her family. Behind a cornfield, about a twenty-minute walk from the studio, stood a desolate farmhouse. There was no kitchen, no bathroom or running water. A small well with a rusty pump lay at the far end of the yard. Lin was helping his mother carry a bucket of water into the house to clean the floor, a slingshot in his hand. He wanted to be prepared, explained Yun, just in case. But of course no one could really be prepared for what was coming.

There were no more fishing trips after that day, although we still got together early in the morning, as much out of habit as out of camaraderie. Quite a few times Baba came with us before leaving for his meetings—for he and Uncle Chen were close friends. Grownups now spoke in hushed voices, even though the next house was an acre away.

"Why are they doing this to Uncle Chen?" I asked Baba.

"Don't believe what you hear," he responded, "and be very careful about what you say."

What a difference from the days, not too long ago, when he'd spoken with hearty confidence about everything. Now doubts, confusion, and caution filled his voice. "Take care of your mom," Baba said, turning to Yun and Lin. "I'll come and visit as soon as I can get away."

The day I had feared finally arrived. Loudspeakers, well positioned all around the studio, blasted out Uncle Chen's name and alleged crimes. Everyone was ordered to be present at a noon meeting, the first of its kind in the studio. Shivering at the memory of similar-sounding meetings I had been to at the language school, I ran to Yun's house.

"Don't go," I pleaded. "Please don't go."

Yun looked like she had been crying. Lin was busy adjusting

his slingshot. Spread on his bunk bed were large stones he must have picked up from around the lake.

"If they dare hurt our father," Yun said, "Lin will fight back." The loudspeakers blasted again. Even from this distance, we could hear everything.

"Let's go," Lin said as he picked up the stones.

The center of the basketball court had been turned into a temporary platform. The soldiers had made good use of the studio's collection of electronics. Four loudspeakers were suspended from the corners of the stage, with a long-necked microphone standing in the front. As the crowd gasped, Uncle Chen, together with two vice presidents of the studio, was pushed out onto the stage. Around each of their necks hung a heavy wooden plaque with the man's name written upside down and a black X over it. The loudspeakers began blasting their names while the soldiers started yelling.

"Lower your heads and confess your crime." One of them tried to force Uncle Chen's head down, but he held it high, with veins bulging and bloody marks around the rope that held the wooden plaque.

"I did *not* commit any crime," Uncle Chen shouted back. "I joined the army at fourteen and fought for China. Is that a crime?"

A red-faced soldier slapped Uncle Chen, hard, and blood mixed with sweat streamed down his face. Yun was trying her best to muffle her sobs, while next to me, Lin, his eyes fixed on the soldier, silently took the slingshot out of his pocket. He

placed a large stone in the center. I thought about the accusa-
tions and threats Lao Lao had been forced to endure as a result
of my little skirmish with the Red Guards. I knew Lin was a
good shot, but what could he gain? Uncle Chen would probably
be beaten to death on account of his son's bravery. I reached out
and jerked the slingshot toward me. Lin's hand let go. He turned
to me in disbelief, but I was already backing up and running,
clutching his slingshot in my hand. Stunned, my two friends ran
after me. I did not stop until I burst into my room and collapsed
onto my bed.

Lin was furious. "Why?" he demanded. I told him about Lao
Lao and the poster and what Di Di and I had done. "You don't
want your dad to be beaten even more because of you," I said.

When he heard this, Lin's broad shoulders began to quiver.
He slumped to the floor and buried his head in his arms. Yun
and I huddled beside him as the room darkened around us. We
wondered what would be next.

The nightmare would not end soon. A few days later, Baba
suddenly appeared during the middle of the day. He closed the
door to his room without a word. Something was very wrong
again. "What happened?" I asked, following him in.

Looking out of the window, he whispered, "They found Uncle Tang hanging from a tree next to the boiler room."

I could not move. Uncle Tang was another good friend of
Baba's, and his daughter was my friend as well. A prominent
movie director, Uncle Tang was famous throughout the country.
Within the studio, he and his wife were known as two lovebirds

who could not bear to be apart. Whenever Uncle Tang had to travel, his wife would carefully pack his suitcase with matching shirts and pants, as well as medicines in small bottles marked for each day he would be away. Then, even after eighteen years of marriage, they would write to each other every day.

Recently, however, Uncle Tang had been branded a traitor. The studio alleged that he had betrayed the Party when he was captured by the Nationalists during the civil war. This was a crime against the country, the studio said. There would be dire consequences for anyone affiliated with him. In the past, an alleged crime of this nature would have led either to prison or to a firing squad. The new head of the studio urged Mrs. Tang to leave her husband in order to show her loyalty to the Party and spare herself. Finally, in desperation, Mrs. Tang decided to ask her husband for a divorce.

"If you insist," Uncle Tang said, "I'll kill myself. There will be nothing else for me to live for." Mrs. Tang insisted, and the following day, they found Uncle Tang dangling from a tree.

Uncle Tang's death hit me harder than all the other events that had swept in and out of my life during the past two years. Maybe it was because he was the first to die among the people I was close to. His death also brought into focus questions that had disturbed me since the beginning of the Cultural Revolution. What's happening to us? I kept asking myself. Why did so many people have to die?

All of life's principles so carefully instilled in me by my parents and reinforced by school and society seemed to have been suddenly turned upside down. Friends became enemies, love turned into hatred. Heaven and hell seemed to have switched places. Now I felt confused, vulnerable, and deeply saddened—feelings that had been totally foreign to me just a few years ago.

I asked Baba to explain all this one night after Uncle Tang's suicide. His usual lightheartedness had been replaced by heavy silence.

"Why did Uncle Tang kill himself? Is he *really* an enemy?"

"No." Then there was silence again.

Tears welled up in my eyes as I thought about Uncle Tang's daughter, my now fatherless friend.

"Uncle Tang was a good man. I knew him well," Baba said, squashing his cigarette in the ashtray. "Just because they accused him of a crime doesn't mean he committed one." Then, before leaving the room, he added, "Don't always believe what people say."

Lately Baba often seemed to be cautioning me not to believe what others said. Unlike the days when I was little, I realized, I could no longer trust grownups with all my heart. Back then, I had learned to be loyal to my family and friends, to trust my teachers and my school, and to be faithful to Chairman Mao and our country. To me, family and country were the same. I had no problem being loyal to both of them.

In the past, our country's enemies had appeared as black and white as my own loyalties. Sometimes, the government had referred to them as the "American imperialists." Other times, our archenemy changed to "Soviet revisionists." These enemies, to me, were far away and easy to hate. Even those at home—the landlords and spies—seemed simple enough for me to detest, since I did not know any of them personally. But now, enemies and friends were no longer that easy to tell apart. To be loyal to one's family, as with Mrs. Tang, would mean to be disloyal to the Party. Sympathizing with one's friends might be perceived as disobeying Chairman Mao. Nowadays, I felt like a child lost in a dense forest, with darkness shrouding every familiar path.

My confusion intensified when, suddenly one day, the loudspeaker in the studio blasted out Baba's name—calling *him* an enemy of the people. Just that day, Baba and a few others had been asked to decorate the assembly hall in order to celebrate the announcement of a new teaching by Chairman Mao. At the time it was popular to make paper cutouts of Mao's image to hang on the wall. Baba was having trouble cutting through the paper. "It's like cutting meat with a dull knife," he had joked.

Not long after, the loudspeaker shouted out his name. "A new counterrevolutionary hides among us. He has dared to make fun of Chairman Mao! We will gather this afternoon for our denunciation meeting."

Someone had betrayed Baba for his innocent comment! Now I wished *I* had Lin's slingshot. That night, when Baba was detained by the soldiers, Lin and Yun, along with their mother, came to see Di Di and me. Mrs. Chen told us that denouncing Baba because of his innocent joke was just a pretense. The studio had been after him for a long time and was simply waiting for an excuse to act. Bringing with them a basket filled with food, Lin and Yun spent the night with Di Di and me in silent solidarity.

Feeling his persecution would be inevitable, Baba called Lao Lao and asked her to take us back to her house again—the army studio was no longer safe for us.

Was there any place that was?

抄家

House Search

HE DAYS OF THE CULTURAL REVOLUTION TICKED AWAY LIKE MINUTES ON A FACELESS CLOCK. SOON IT WAS HARD TO REMEMBER WHAT LIFE HAD been like before the Red Guards. We lived from one hour to the next.

After Baba was detained at the movie studio, Di Di and I returned home to stay with Lao Lao. I was relieved to find our house untouched. Lao Lao, as usual, had dusted every piece of furniture meticulously, and the bookcases stood there as always—our silent guardians—extending from floor to ceiling one after another.

There was nothing Baba treasured more than his books. He spent every penny saved from his meager salary on them. He even designed a special bookcase for Di Di and me, made of redwood and framed with beautiful glass panels. On the shelves, he lined up world literature that he had carefully selected for us—from Andersen's fairy tales to Aesop's fables, from Mark Twain's stories to Jack London's *The Call of the Wild*.

Baba had taught Di Di and me to wrap each book with a fresh paper cover, like dressing up a child in new clothes. He told us that the rare books he had been collecting—those bound in rice paper and tied with silk strings—would be available to us when we were old enough to understand and appreciate them.

Often at night after dinner, Baba would pull out one of our favorite books from the shelf, flip to the page where we had last stopped, and curl up on the sofa with us. At first, Baba read to us. Then, as we grew older, Di Di and I took turns reading out loud. Di Di liked *The Call of the Wild*, and so we read it together several times. Any word we did not know, we'd run to Baba's desk and look up in the thick dictionary lying open there. It was our family ritual.

Baba's love of books was in his blood, Mama said, since he had descended from a long line of bookworms. Some of his relatives, such as my great-grandfather and grand-uncle, had worked their way through the last phase of the imperial examination system with flying colors before it was abolished. This family legacy continued with my grandfather's generation. All the siblings—eight brothers and three sisters—graduated from college, quite an accomplishment at the time. Each of them, later on, managed to make a dent in contemporary Chinese history.

Following this family tradition, Baba had been sent to school at age five and was given a heavy dose of the classics. His father, my Ye Ye, was dean of civil engineering at Beijing University. Ye Ye tried but failed to get his oldest son interested in anything beyond the humanities.

When he was in high school, however, Baba's education was

interrupted by war. Japanese troops had marched into Beijing in 1937, when Baba was only seven years old. There was nothing worse, he told me, than watching your country be destroyed by a ruthless conqueror. The Japanese posted signs everywhere that read NO CHINESE OR DOGS ALLOWED. In school, he and his friends vowed to save China from the aggressors when they grew up.

And so, at fourteen, Baba joined the underground resistance. In the meantime, my Ye Ye had enraged the authorities by turning down a lucrative position as a protest against the government's corruption. As a result, the entire family had to move out of Beijing for safety. They were welcomed into the arms of Mao's troops farther north. There, Baba became a soldier.

The army, Baba soon found out, also valued bookworms. Not long after he joined their ranks, Baba was called into his commander's office. "I know you've had a high school education and are good with words," he said, "a very valuable thing to us. We'd like you to continue your education in the army." At the time, many universities had relocated away from big cities because of the war, setting up temporary campuses in unoccupied territories. Baba decided to enroll in the Department of Literature at Huabei Union College, not far from where his division was stationed. Two years later, in 1947, he graduated. Immediately he was sent to join an artillery unit in the final battles for a new China. In 1949, Baba rolled back into Beijing in his tank— a proud member of the liberating forces.

The army, however, had not forgotten its investment in

Baba in his teens as a soldier, in front of a dedication flag

Baba. In the early 1960s, he was assigned to work for their movie studio as a screenwriter. There, he was expected to combine his life as a soldier with his training as a writer. This assignment allowed Baba once again to return to his old friends—books—for wisdom and understanding. Knowledge and education, he never tired of telling me, were as important to a person as they were to a nation.

∽

From Baba I learned to value books. But I never truly appreciated them until one day in 1968 shortly after I had returned home from the movie studio. That day I left early to visit my friend Wen, whose father had been taken away. The little hideout at the back of their yard and his four girls, armed with all the weapons they could find in and around their house—clubs, stones, cracked bricks, and broken chairs—had failed to protect him.

By sheer will, Wen and her sisters were able to keep the Red Guards away from their father's hideout for hours—until Red Guard reinforcements arrived. Then their father, equally brave, forced his way out and gave himself up to protect his children. The Red Guards eventually took Wen's second-oldest sister with them, her clothes torn to shreds and her hands and feet tightly bound with heavy ropes. She simply refused to give up and threatened all who dared to come close to her. Neither her father's pleas nor the Red Guards' clubs could stop her.

Their house was ravaged by angry Red Guards, and nothing

was left standing. When I arrived the following day, smoke from burnt books and furniture was still lingering in the air. No one was crying. No one seemed scared. Wen and her sisters sat there like warriors—enraged by their defeat but ready for battle again.

"Come and stay with me," I said, pulling Wen's hand, "at least for a few days." She stared at me as if from a thousand miles away. "Come," I pleaded again. She seemed startled and shook her head vehemently.

"Go," urged Ling, her oldest sister. "Go with her."

Ling signaled me with a nod and together we held on to Wen's arms and half pushed and pulled her out of the shattered house. As soon as we were outside the door, Wen collapsed. I wrapped my arms around her as she sobbed, and we sat there, huddled together, until she quieted down. Finally she agreed to come with me. We held on to each other's arms and walked for two long hours through the Beijing streets until we reached my house, our tears drying along the way.

But when we pushed the door open and stepped inside, it was like leaving one horror movie only to find ourselves in another. Broken furniture, torn-up books, scattered paper, and fragments of phonograph records were everywhere. The two records that Mama loved most—Strauss's *Blue Danube* Waltz and Vivaldi's *Four Seasons*—lay in jagged pieces on the floor, along with all our other records. Lao Lao was on her knees trying to pick up the fragments, her hands trembling.

After Wen and I helped Lao Lao to her feet and sat her down, she told us what had happened. The soldiers had arrived in a truck with Baba. They dragged him into our house before they rummaged through all our things.

"*Blue Danube?*" one of them said, picking up the phonograph record from the turntable. "Don't you know all bourgeois music has been banned?" Whacking it against a wooden bench, he shattered it. Then he smashed record after record, until hundreds of tiny pieces littered the floor.

Another soldier searched all our drawers and confiscated everything—including my little bankbook, with thirty yuan ($3.50) recorded in it. It had taken me over two years to save that much from my monthly two-yuan allowance.

In front of Baba's eyes, they flung book after book onto the stone floor. One of them reached into a lower shelf for Baba's rare books. Dragging them out by their silk strings, he yanked them open.

"Please," Baba pleaded, trying to free himself from the hands of his guard. "Don't touch those."

The guard pulled Baba's arms back and tied a rope around them.

Then the soldiers dumped all our books into large hemp sacks that they pulled from the back of the truck. "The paper factory will turn this trash into pulp in no time," they announced. When Lao Lao tried to plead with them, a soldier just pushed her away. Dragging the sacks through our gate, they flung them, one after another, onto the open truck. Then, hurling Baba on top of the bulging bags, the soldiers drove away in a cloud of dust, leaving my grandmother filled with sorrow.

Lao Lao dried her eyes with a handkerchief. My friend Ming and a few other neighbors had come to help. "Take Lao Lao back to her room, please," Ming's mother said to him. Together with Wen, Ming helped Lao Lao to her feet and led her slowly away.

With our neighbors' help, I cleared the rubble. After everyone had left, I closed the door and all the windows and sank to the cold stone floor, my face buried in my arms. The sun was setting, and darkness was creeping into the house. Our bookshelves now stood naked in the shadows—like proud but defeated old warriors.

内蒙古旋曲
Mongolian Melody

Y THE SUMMER OF 1970, MY FAVORITE COUSIN, LEE, HAD BEEN WORKING IN A REMOTE MOUNTAIN VILLAGE IN INNER MONGOLIA FOR ALMOST TWO years. Recently, she had been diagnosed with a serious heart defect and soon would be returning home for good. Where she lived, there was no adequate medical care. When she heard about what had happened to my parents, she invited me to visit her—"to get away from the city," she wrote, "even if it's just for a little while."

By now, lots of teenagers only a few years older than I had been sent to the distant countryside, as Mao had instructed. He believed that students and intellectuals needed to be "reeducated" by the peasants so that they wouldn't be led astray by what they learned at school. Wen's sister Ling, after the failed battle to save her father, had joined a large group of juniors and seniors from our high school bound for Heilongjiang, which borders Russia. She rarely wrote home, and even when she did the letters were always short. "It means she is going through hard times," Wen told me knowingly, "but she doesn't want my parents to worry." My cousin Lee did not write often, either.

I had wondered what life was like for Ling and my cousin. So I accepted Lee's invitation, bought a cheap train ticket for a wooden bench seat, and embarked on a daylong journey north.

The scenery started to change quickly after we pulled out of Beijing, with gray city apartments giving way to well-tended rice paddies. Farmers with wide straw hats squatted in the fields under the scorching sun. Only one-third of all the land in China is arable; every square inch counts. As the long hours passed, the soil became more and more yellow, and fewer and fewer trees dotted the horizon. Rolling hills, mostly barren, loomed in the distance.

Finally the train chugged into a dusty city, a major outpost of Inner Mongolia—Baotou. I followed the small crowd off the train, my feet numb from sitting on the hard seat for so long. I was happy to see my cousin Lee waving from the platform—she was someone you could always count on.

Lee looked even taller than I remembered but much thinner. Her hair was sandy brown, like the soil, carelessly tied into two short ponytails. Lee had been the first among my cousins to chop off her beautiful waist-length braids at the beginning of the Cultural Revolution. She had very fair skin, big brown eyes, and long lashes, shared by quite a few relatives on my mama's side. Now she was tanned like a bronze statue and looked just like the locals. Only her light brown eyes gave her away.

Behind her stood a short, barefoot young farmer, holding an old donkey by a rope. "Our village is still twenty miles away," Lee said. "So we brought along the only form of transportation the village could spare in case our city guest could not manage the long journey."

"You've underestimated me," I tried to explain. "Hiking ten to twenty miles for military training at school is common practice these days." I remembered how our school, when it was open, had organized long marches for us to various destinations. Sometimes our goal had been to visit an old revolutionary site and listen to the locals recall the good old days when they assisted the army in fighting the Japanese. Other times it was to see the villages where some of Mao's heroes had lived and died.

Little by little our blistered feet were hardened into "iron feet." To lift our spirits along the way, we would sing heartwarming revolutionary songs. No one complained. At least no one dared to. When our lead teacher shouted, "Are you tired?" we always shouted back in unison, "Not tired." He would then say, "It's not true that you are not tired. But your spirit is never tired." He was a predictable man, and we were predictable students. Today, in Inner Mongolia, I could once again test my marching skills.

We did cheat with the luggage, though, by loading it on the old donkey. Back in Beijing, our teachers would have insisted that we carry it as part of our training. In Baotou, we decided to put the donkey to good use.

We set off on the yellow dirt road. Because I had grown up

in the city, just seeing a goat or a horse by the roadside made me gasp. From time to time, I stooped to pick yellow daisies, hardy flowers that managed to survive between cracked rocks. I put one in my cousin's hair. She smiled indulgently. Lee was only three years older than I, but she had always behaved like my grownup guardian. A star student at a prestigious girls' school before the Cultural Revolution, she excelled in both the sciences and the humanities. I thought she was destined for something big—to become a scientist, maybe even a Nobel Prize winner.

"What's your day like here?" I asked.

"You'll find out soon enough," she replied.

We were climbing a hill along a narrow footpath. By now several hours had passed since we had started, but I was managing to keep up. My school training was paying off. So was our donkey. The young farmer was very quiet the whole way, only giving yes and no answers to all my questions.

"He is very shy," Lee explained. "He'll warm up once he gets to know you. Let's take a break here."

Now we were on top of a large boulder where, amazingly, it was quite flat and even a little grassy. I could tell the donkey needed a break, and so did I. My legs were getting tired, and I could feel blisters on my feet. The young farmer stretched out on the grass and covered his face with his straw hat. I looked at his bare feet. No doubt he had had a lot more training than I— his feet must have been truly made of iron.

"What's his story?" I asked my cousin, leaning back against a big rock.

"There are three boys in his family. No one is married because they are too poor to afford brides. The brothers have agreed that they'll work together to earn enough money for the oldest one to marry, then the next. Here, if you can't afford to pay the matchmaker and provide enough gifts to the bride's family, no parents will let their daughter marry you. It's been two years since the brothers made the pact. Still, they haven't scraped together enough money for even the oldest brother to marry. He is already twenty-five years old—over the hill by local standards. I'm paying this youngest brother two yuan [twenty-five cents] to come with me to pick you up. That's a lot of money to them."

Finally, as the sun was setting, we reached Lee's village, nestled halfway up the mountain. I was exhausted but proud that I had made it on my own. People here lived in cave houses dug into the steep sides of the hills, where it was cool and dry during the summer and warm during the winter. There was no electricity or running water, and the windows were covered with rice paper. The bed, or *kang*, was made of clay, hollow in its core, where heat from the cooking stove, connected to it by an exhaust pipe from the adjacent kitchen, would keep it warm during the winter. During the summer, cooking was done on an open stove in the communal yard. I was impressed by the natural, energy-saving heating system. Smart farmers, I thought. Apparently we did have a lot to learn from them—just as Chairman Mao had told us.

My cousin started a fire in the open stove outside and made some delicious egg noodle soup, thanks to the chickens she raised, which were roaming the yard like proud queens.

Several of her friends, all fellow Beijing students, stopped by, bearing presents for us—pears, dates, yams, and eggs. Some local farmers came to visit, too. No one came empty-handed. Even the head of the village made a point of stopping by. Unlike everyone else, he was smartly dressed in a brand-new white polyester shirt. One sleeve was rolled up to show off his gleaming new watch. He did not have much to say, but he laughed a lot. I had some trouble understanding his dialect and thought I must have missed the joke completely. No one else was laughing either, however.

"You didn't miss anything," Lee said to me knowingly. "He considers himself the king of the village, and he is, to a certain extent; he holds our future in his hands. The white shirt and the watch were gifts from a student, in an effort to bribe his way out of this village."

My cousin's house was spartan, with a beat-up desk that served as a dining table, study desk, and workbench. A small chest of drawers stood in the corner—the only other furniture besides two benches and the clay bed. Lee pulled out a washed-out blanket from the chest of drawers for me. I was tired from the journey and went right to sleep.

∽

High-pitched crows from Lee's roosters woke me in the morning, followed by the voices of our neighbors' roosters. It was like being surrounded by a rooster orchestra. The old alarm clock on the desk pointed its hour hand at five. Rise and shine, I thought. I got out of bed and walked into the yard.

Lee was up already. Looking around, I saw smoke coming out of many stoves. "This is the beginning of our daily routine," she said. Barley porridge and corn bread with pickles for breakfast was another daily routine. Unlike in Beijing, there was no rice here.

"Let me help you carry water back from the well," I volunteered after breakfast.

"Are you sure you can handle it? There's a lot of uphill walking."

"I've done it before, when we were helping farmers during harvest," I assured her.

The local well was two miles down the hill. All the villagers, about a hundred of them, went there every morning to carry water home in two big pails each, well balanced on their shoulders. The way down to the well was easy, even though the pails were much bigger than the ones I had carried before. Throwing the wooden pail into the deep well took practice. A rope was tied to a timber beam across the well, and the pail was loosely hooked onto the other end and slowly lowered. Giving it the right swing would tilt it just enough to catch water. Too much angle or too hard a swing might knock the pail over and sink it. I had lost such a pail myself trying to help the farmers during one of the harvests. So this time I handed the pail to my more experienced cousin.

After Lee filled both containers, I balanced them over the long bamboo pole, trying to remember how I had done this before. The wooden pails felt much heavier than I recalled, and my balancing was not as good as I remembered, either. My cousin knew me too well to intervene and walked close by just in case. The first few yards were not bad, but then I started to feel the full weight of the water. I gritted my teeth and steadied my pace. A village girl a few years younger than I passed by us with the same load on her shoulders. She looked like she was simply out for a walk. I bit my lip this time and doubled my efforts. I did not last as long as I had hoped before my cousin forced me to stop and let her take over.

"You've done very well already. Save some strength for to-morrow," she said.

After a simple dinner of corn bread and stir-fried cabbage, Lee and I relaxed on the wooden bench in her yard. "I've heard about what happened in Beijing," she finally said. "It must be aw-ful for you."

As we sat in this quiet village yard and watched the distant hills slowly disappear in the darkness, all the terrible things that had happened during the past four years passed through my mind, like a movie in slow motion.

I told Lee about how our home was ransacked by soldiers and how Baba was taken away, about Uncle Tang dangling from a tree at the movie studio, and about Uncle Chen with his head held high and a heavy wooden plaque around his neck. I also told her about my headmaster ending his life on Fragrant Hill, and the deputy headmaster's daughter with her stick. And I told her about Lan—how she had helped raise the little girl's hand.

Lee let out a deep sigh. "Our headmaster was beaten, too,"

she said, "right in front of my eyes. Even though I wasn't the one with the stick in my hand, I was one of the Red Guards there, supporting the whole thing."

Lee, my gentle cousin. I looked at her in disbelief.

"I know how Lan must have felt," Lee said, avoiding my eyes, "with her blood rushing and her heart pounding fast. At the time I *did* believe that our headmaster was an enemy of the people and that by teaching him a lesson we were defending Chairman Mao."

After a long pause, Lee continued, lowering her head. "Now, after living here on this desolate mountain for so long, I'm not sure of anything."

∽

A heavy downpour mixed with lightning and thunder woke me the following morning. I saw my cousin standing in front of the window, looking worried. "A rain like this is the worst possible thing this time of year, a few months short of harvesttime."

"Why?"

"You'll see."

The rain came down all day, never losing its force. It was as if the sky was in a rage and wanted to punish the earth by dumping all the water it could. Finally, before darkness engulfed the village, the rain tapered off. At the first sign of clearing, we ran out the door.

The village's farmland was scattered all around the terraces of the mountain, taking whatever shape the slope naturally offered. Some pieces were no bigger than my cousin's backyard. "Good soil is precious here," she told me. "The growing season is short and the winters long. Wheat and barley are primary staples. There are no tractors, or any other kind of machinery, just old cows, plows, and the backs of the students and the local farmers themselves."

Several villagers walking up the hill passed by us with tears in their eyes. We picked up our speed. Halfway down to the lower slope, I understood. The torrential rain had washed away a big section of the barley field.

"The villagers have been at nature's mercy since the beginning of time," said Lee. "Each year, the rain takes some land away and, sometimes, their homes, too. Then they move to higher ground."

That explained why there were so many abandoned caves on the lower slopes, looking like ghost towns. "Why don't you try to harness the water, turn it into electricity, and apply scientific agriculture to this place?" I asked. "You were a science star in your school."

My cousin gave me a resigned smile. "We all came here with those dreams. I even brought some books with me so I could study further. But pretty soon, the necessity of survival takes over, and the daily grind becomes routine."

"I'm sorry," I mumbled, feeling ashamed of my presumption. I had been here for only two days. We turned around and walked back up the hill with the rest of the villagers. No one uttered a word the whole way.

As we approached Lee's house, I saw the flickering light of a kerosene lamp; we had a visitor. A tall young man in a worn blue jacket stood up to greet us. "I'm sorry to have barged in like this; the door was open," he said in a soft, deep voice.

My cousin blushed. Why hadn't I seen him the first night? He must have been the one everybody else was asking about when my cousin was cooking outside. I liked him right away. Broad-shouldered and well tanned, he had something solid yet gentle about him.

Most of the students in this village had come from Beijing—as part of the very first group from big cities. They all had been enthusiastic volunteers answering the call of Chairman Mao, humbly eager to be reeducated by the peasants. Unlike many others who followed less willingly later, this group was made up of true idealists.

Lee went out to cook again, as the young man, Peng, skillfully fanned the stove to get the flames higher. They talked in soft, low voices. From time to time, Peng would wrap his arm around Lee's shoulders.

During dinner, I asked Peng, "Are you going back to Beijing with Lee?"

A tight smile crossed his face. "My father is still in prison, and my prospect of ever getting out of here is dim."

Wrong question.

"Peng plays the flute well," Lee said, breaking the awkward silence that followed. She opened the chest of drawers and took out a beautiful bamboo flute, while Peng stood up and smiled at her. Then, he took a deep breath.

From the flute came a sweet, sad melody, "Liangzhu"—a popular tune with lyrics based on a story similar to *Romeo and Juliet*—written some seven hundred years before Shakespeare made his own hero and heroine timeless.

Like Romeo and Juliet, Liang Shanbo and Zhu Yingtai fall in love and vow to marry no one else but each other. Zhu Yingtai's family, however, has promised her to another man without her knowledge, and a wedding day is set. When he hears the sad news, Liang Shanbo's failing health takes a sudden turn for the worse, and he dies before his true love can reach him. In sorrow and desperation, Zhu Yingtai orders her wedding chair to stop in front of Liang's tomb. There she cries out for him. With a roar, the tomb cracks open, and the heroine walks straight in before it closes again behind her. Afterward, two beautiful butterflies circle the tomb day and night.

I watched as Lee lowered her head, away from the glow of the lamp. Were my cousin and Peng also doomed to be star-crossed lovers? I shuddered at the thought.

Secret Reading Club

HINESE NEW YEAR WAS MY FAVORITE HOLIDAY, BUT NOT IN 1970. ON THAT NEW YEAR'S EVE, DI DI AND I SLOUCHED IN THE CORNER OF OUR DIMLY lit living room, half asleep. Lao Lao and our other relatives huddled around the stove and talked in hushed voices. From time to time, I would glance at the door.

In the past, our New Year's Day had been a time of celebration and feasting. It was a day when the oldest, and especially the youngest, were spoiled with gifts from members of our extended family. At least twenty guests—including relatives, friends, and friends of friends—usually shared the occasion with us. The female members of the family, with Lao Lao in charge, would cook the whole day—filling our kitchen with giggles and laughter and the fragrant smells of pork stew, chicken soup, spicy tofu, and juicy dumplings. Di Di and I, together with our cousins and friends, would sneak in and out of the kitchen in a collective effort to sample the delicacies before they were served. At Lao

Lao's house, the dining table would be extended to the full length of the sitting room—every square inch covered with delicious dishes. The first toast would be made to Lao Lao for good health and long life, followed by joking toasts for everyone else. After dinner, we would all urge my youngest auntie to sing while Da Jiu accompanied her on his flute. Sometimes we even talked Lao Lao into picking up her bamboo lute.

New Year's Eve was also the only time of the year when children were allowed to stay up past midnight. Dressed in our New Year's best, we would parade through the neighborhood with our red lanterns, made of rice paper and shaped like the moon or the stars. Suspended from bamboo sticks and illuminated by tiny candles inside, these lanterns twinkled in the dark night like the Milky Way on earth. When the clock struck twelve, fireworks from neighborhoods all across the city would go off—sending up burst after burst of colorful explosions, each one higher and brighter than the last as they illuminated the Beijing sky.

This New Year, however, there were no gifts or firecrackers in our house, and cooking was reduced to a minimum. Mama was still confined at her school, and Baba had been taken to a hard labor camp far, far away, in Shanxi, where the winter was even harsher than in Beijing. Our family had lost its soul.

Friends and relatives did come, but the conversation was hushed and serious. By now, everyone was affected by the Cultural Revolution in one way or another. Nearly every family we knew had lost someone to a labor camp. No one seemed to know what would happen next. Rumors about the politically powerful and their private lives, stories one could not get from official government channels, had become our main course and dessert.

In the midst of this quiet conversation came a soft knock on the door. Lao Lao hurried over and peeked through the edge of our curtain. "It's your *baba*'s friend, Uncle Lu," she said, opening the door wide. Di Di and I were jolted back to life. Would he have word of Baba? While Lao Lao poured him a steaming cup of jasmine tea, we gathered around Uncle Lu.

"You've both grown taller," he said, looking us over from head to toe. Then, carefully, he unbuttoned his green cotton jacket, and from an inside pocket, he produced a folded envelope. It was sealed. By now, we had grown used to receiving our letters already opened, for all to see. Every letter in or out of Baba's labor camp was scrutinized by the security guards. Baba had stopped bothering to seal his, which saved him some glue and the army guards some effort.

This time was different. We knew the letter carried out secretly by Uncle Lu must be important. I unfolded the thick dark-brown envelope, peeled back its flap, and carefully pulled out three thin pieces of paper: it was a reading list.

"Even though school is not teaching you much, and all our books were taken away," Baba wrote, "I want you to try to educate yourselves."

On Baba's list were some two dozen books—ranging from Russian and British to American literature. Almost all of them were currently banned. Next to each title, he had indicated where we could find it. For Shakespeare, he wrote, "Find Uncle Gu. He has Shakespeare's plays in both English and Chinese. Compare them as you read, since they were written by the best and translated by the best as well."

"For *Anna Karenina*," Baba continued, "go to Uncle He. For Mark Twain, call Aunt Liu. Make sure you read each book carefully, and don't give up. I know you can do it."

Huddled under the shade of the dim table lamp, Di Di and I read Baba's letter over and over before passing it on to the rest of the family. It seemed like this was his New Year's gift to us. Looking at our bookshelves, now empty, I could almost see Baba—fingering through his precious collection, as he did so often, and carefully pulling out *The Call of the Wild* as Di Di and I curled up next to him for our favorite family pastime—reading together.

The very next day, I hurried to call on Uncle Gu and came home with a bag bulging with works of Shakespeare—my first reading assignment on Baba's long list. Setting my bag down on the floor, I took a minute to nurse my shoulder, tender from carrying the weight for so long. Uncle Gu lived far away. It had taken me an hour by bus and another half hour on foot to get to his house.

I lined the books up on our shelves the way Baba used to do. It had been almost two years since our collection had been taken away. Surprisingly, the empty space on these shelves seemed even more obvious with the presence of a few books, especially under the soft light of the green reading lamp on Baba's desk.

I sat down at the desk and adjusted the light, which used to cast Baba's long shadow against the wall, a shadow that had been comforting when I sometimes woke up late at night and found him still buried in his books. Now, looking back at the wall, I saw a smaller shadow—my own.

There was no order or logic to my first encounter with Shakespeare. I picked up one of two Chinese translations I had brought back with me this visit. It happened to be *King Lear*. I chose the slightly easier road, reading the Chinese version first. Then I laid it side by side with its English counterpart and, an index finger on each page, read the original English text slowly. It was hard going. Even though I had started English at age nine, the Cultural Revolution had cut my studies short three years later. School had been on and off since then, and the only book we were allowed to study in English was Mao's Little Red Book. From Mao to Shakespeare was a big jump, but I struggled along.

Baba used to say that accumulating knowledge was, sometimes, like feeding a camel. The camel took in all its food at one time and then stored it in its hump as fuel and energy for the long journey ahead. It might take the camel days or weeks to digest what was put in, but what it absorbed eventually served as essential nutrients for the body, the heart, and the mind. I felt a strange affinity with this king of the desert as I plowed through Baba's reading list.

Shakespeare went into my system the same way other, lesser minds did, pretty much undigested, even though here and there a familiar note struck me at some unexpected moment. "Speak what we feel, not what we ought to say," announced Edgar as a final reflection on the love and betrayal experienced by the unfortunate King Lear. "The oldest has borne most: we that are young shall never see so much, nor live so long."

Following the tragedy of King Lear, I slowly drifted out of my world and time into a remote era and place, spellbound by the king's fate and suffering—a fate both strange and familiar. Loyalty and betrayal, honesty and deception—all of this had become so very recognizable in my own world. These flickers of insights were buried as quickly as the rest of my reading material, all in an unrecognizable lump, the hump on my back, for a later date.

Mark Twain and his characters were less of a struggle. I felt a strange bond with Tom Sawyer and Huckleberry Finn. These teenage characters turned adversity into adventure. With his irreverent humor and reverent heart, Mark Twain offered me my own passport for adventure—the adventure of the mind, separating the world of reality from the world of the imagination. In his world, I felt safe and happy.

On his own, Di Di had discovered another source of books. He told me how he and his friends had wandered into a warehouse near their school. In it, buried amid old desks and chairs, were bundles of forbidden literature. Among a dusty pile of books, he had stumbled onto *The Call of the Wild*. Looking around to make sure nobody was watching, he'd tucked it under his jacket. I was so happy when he brought this old friend home!

Later, Di Di told me that he had snuck back into the storage place a few more times, until one day the old gatekeeper spotted him. "What's under your jacket?" he demanded. Hesitantly, Di Di showed him the books.

"I just want to read them," he said. "We've lost all our books."

The old man hesitated, then waved his hand and said, "Go now. I won't report you this time. But don't come back again."

Di Di and I became very secretive about our books and their sources. We didn't want to get Baba's friends in trouble, since foreign literature was forbidden by the government. After displaying them for a few hours on the bookshelf, where they were a reminder of Baba and his own treasured books, I reluctantly took them down and hid them in empty shoe boxes under my bed. Now I only read them at home with Di Di, behind a closed door. But I longed to share this newfound pleasure with my old friend Wen.

By now, Wen had joined the army and was stationed in a mountainous region a few hundred miles from Beijing, where nothing, especially books, was accessible. I had visited her there a few times. The long train ride took me into a remote settlement in the frozen mountains of the Northeast. Throughout history, Wen told me, this place had been considered an important military outpost by both the Mongol horsemen and the Han armies. There, hidden inside the deep hills, was the army hospital where she had been working as a nurse.

Her bedroom was even smaller than ours at the language school, with a narrow single bed, a small metal desk, and an old porcelain washbasin sitting on top of a rusty steel rack. To go to the nearest grocery store, we had to wait for the commuter bus that came only twice a day. Several times during the week, lights would go off in the dormitory in order to save electricity. The only entertainment was an occasional movie, shown outdoors during the short summer. The list of movie titles was as lean as our wallets—the ballet *The Red Detachment of Women*, and the Beijing operas *Capture the Weihu Mountain* and the *Legend of the Red Lantern*. We had watched them so many times that we could recite the lines from memory.

I told Wen about Baba's reading list during one of my visits. She was thrilled. "Count me in," she said. "I'm dying to read something new and fun."

"But what if someone saw you with a banned book?" I asked.

"Don't worry. I'll think of something," she answered.

I trusted her—Wen was always full of clever ideas. To avoid attracting the attention of the army post office, she suggested that I pack a book with a few boxes of cookies and mark FOOD on the lower corner of the parcel. The postmen were used to care packages, since many families sent food to their enlisted children to supplement their skimpy diet. When she opened the package, Wen would slide the book into the red plastic cover from a book by Mao—creating perfect camouflage—and read it only by flashlight at night.

Mark Twain became Wen's favorite, too. She copied down several stories word by word and could soon recall them from memory. During our long walks in the parks when she came to visit me, Wen would mimic Tom Sawyer whitewashing his aunt's fence, his friends begging to swap their treasures with him for a chance at the chore. With her hands in the air and her eyes bright, Wen became her old self again. Since her home had been destroyed and her father taken away by the Red Guards, Wen had retreated inside herself. A soldier now at sixteen, she walked and talked like a serious adult. But Tom Sawyer made her laugh again like a child.

∽

One day I welcomed into my secret reading club a rather unlikely candidate—my old elementary school teacher Miss Chen. I often visited her during the holidays. Teacher Chen lived in a small one-bedroom apartment on our school campus with her husband, a teacher of Chinese, and their two young boys. A large portrait of Chairman Mao on the wall completed the interior decoration, as it did in most other Chinese households. The parents' room served as bedroom, living room, and makeshift dining area.

When I went to see her one day, I noticed, in the already cramped parents' quarters, a new piece of furniture. It was a handmade chest of drawers, placed at an odd angle to their bed. My puzzled look must have amused Teacher Chen, and she motioned me into the room before closing the door behind her.

"Let me show you something," she said. Carefully, she unlocked the cabinet that was part of the chest. "I've been writing plays and short stories," she explained. "Some of them are based on fairy tales and mythology, like those I used to tell you in third and fourth grade, not permitted anymore these days."

This brought back a vivid memory of performing *Little Red Riding Hood* in her class. I remembered putting on the red velvet cape, hand-stitched by Teacher Chen.

"Please keep on writing. Children today will love your stories as much as we did," I said.

"I must be careful not to cause trouble again," she said with a sigh. "Remember how I was blamed for polluting your minds with foreign fairy tales?"

I shuddered, recalling the stark posters that had suddenly appeared, questioning her loyalty.

"With this new furniture, I can push the desk in and close the cabinet to the chest of drawers as soon as I hear someone coming, so no one will suspect," she said. "You know how some people just wander into your house unannounced," she added with a wry smile. Opening her drawer, she pulled out a large pile of manuscripts. "I've never shown them to anyone outside this family. But now you know."

I did not quite know what to say. Then I found myself confessing, "I've something to tell you, too. For some time now I've been reading from a list sent to me by my *baba*, with books borrowed from his friends. It is mostly classic foreign literature, such as Shakespeare and Mark Twain. Baba asked me to keep it to myself in order to avoid causing anyone trouble."

Teacher Chen gave me a knowing smile. "I still have a few of Mark Twain's stories myself," she said, "even though I don't have much else. You're welcome to them."

From that day on, Teacher Chen joined my reading club. I

would simply bring books to her when their lending time allowed, and during my visits she would patiently answer any questions I had.

Gradually, I realized that Baba's reading list was offering me more than just a joyful escape. It had given me a new sense of direction. And reading had taken on a meaning of its own. In a small way, I was regaining control of my life. My secret reading club, which never held an official meeting, helped to keep the flame of education alive inside me when the rest of my world was still besieged by darkness.

成年
Coming of Age

N 1971, TWO YEARS AFTER HE HAD BEEN TAKEN AWAY, BABA WAS FINALLY GRANTED A TEMPORARY RELEASE. LATE ONE AFTERNOON, I LOOKED UP and saw him standing in front of me—the frayed uniform hanging loosely on him, his face thin and pale. His eyes lit up, though, as he hugged Di Di and me. "I could eat a cow," he announced in good spirits. "I'll cook today."

Baba had never cooked, although he had wandered into the kitchen from time to time, offering tongue-in-cheek critiques of other people's culinary skills. Since his salary had been reduced, our meals had been cut down to plain cabbage day after day. But today Baba suggested pork stew. What a treat that would be! We went to the market together.

The local food market was as bare as our kitchen cabinet, however. Most of the shelves were empty, with just a few thin pieces of pork sitting pathetically on the butcher's counter. You needed both meat coupons and money to buy it. The vegetable stand looked equally barren, with winter cabbages piled one on top of the other taking over most of the shelf space, accompanied only by some half-frozen scallions. Very few people were in the store. After all, with so little to buy, shopping was made simple, and there were few temptations. Still, as we approached the meat stand, I felt excited.

"Two pounds of pork, please," Baba requested. Happily, the butcher complied. He was an expert butcher—a legend, Lao Lao had told me, known for his cutting skills. With one steady swing of his well-sharpened cleaver, he cut what appeared to be a big chunk out of his limited supply. And it was two pounds even—no more, no less—on the iron scale. The butcher puffed on the cigarette that was tucked between his lips the whole time, and a slow, barely visible smile appeared, then disappeared as quickly as it came.

Back at home, Lao Lao had gone to visit a sick relative, so Baba was left to be the king of the kitchen. I became his sous-chef, helping him wash the scallions and peel the garlic. As I watched, Baba sliced the meat carefully into small chunks.

"When was the last time you had meat?" I asked.

"Well, I don't remember. For as long as I've been away."

Baba stopped chopping and looked at me. "I tried to save some money to buy you a thick cotton quilt. I thought you might be sent to the countryside, where the weather is cold. I hid the money inside my pillowcase, but one day it was gone. I don't know who took it; I couldn't even try to track it down, since the guards might think I was up to something."

Looking at me apologetically, he said, "The pork money is all that was left. But at least today we'll have a good meal together."

Baba dropped a handful of scallions and ginger into the siz-zling oil—*puff!* The kitchen was filled with a pungent smell. Then, carefully, he placed each piece of pork in the wok. He added in spoonfuls of soy sauce and a dash of sugar, and then I stood there next to him, watching the sweet vapor whirl up from the wok. He wrapped his arm around my shoulder, and I felt thick calluses on his hand.

When Baba carried a large white porcelain bowl to the din-ing table, I had already laid spoons, chopsticks, and ceramic rice bowls in place. After searching all our cabinets, Di Di found half a bottle of rice wine, which must have been a leftover gift from the previous New Year.

"Welcome home, Baba," my brother said, raising his wine cup high.

Baba's eyes moistened as he clinked his cup with each of us. Then he smiled. "Come, eat while it's hot." Spoonful after spoonful, he dished the juicy meat into our rice bowls.

I had almost forgotten how delicious stewed pork could be! Before I realized it, I had gobbled down half of the food in my bowl. But when I lifted my head to look at Baba again, he had not touched his. With his elbows resting on the table and his body leaning toward us, he was watching us eat, his eyes smiling.

ဢ

Baba did not talk much about his experience at the labor camp, either in letters or in person. Some of the reports I heard came from his "cell mates," friends who shared a room with Baba behind electric barbed wire. One of my favorite stories was told by Uncle Lu, the friend who had brought us Baba's reading list.

Uncle Lu was a famous actor, and during another of his visits he began his story with a theatrical flair. "It was New Year's Eve. We were all feeling quite depressed. Most of us had not seen our families for a very long time. Ten of us shared a small cave room dug deep into the mountain. In our caves the rats were bigger than cats," Uncle Lu said, extending his hands to show us their size.

"The winter in Shanxi is quite severe. We had only thin blankets on our beds and a small stove that hardly worked. Every day, we were forced to work outside in the freezing temperature—cleaning pigsties by wading through knee-high mud and manure, and digging water channels with heavy pickaxes to break through the ice. Our New Year's dinner was the same old rotten cabbage and spoiled corn bread. They doubled the guards in fear that some of us might get desperate and try to escape. But we were a bunch of battle-hardened war veterans. Most of us had joined the army when we were your age and we fought the Japanese, then the Nationalists. It was not in our nature to run away. However, we sometimes wondered why our lives were spared while so many of our friends died in battle.

"Some of us had been in prison before, except those were Japanese and Nationalist prisons. I guess that is the biggest irony. After surviving enemy prisons, with heads held high, we have now found ourselves imprisoned by our own people. Back then, we were ready and proud to die at any time for what we believed in. Here, if we died, our own people would put our names and families to shame.

"One day a few months ago, one of our friends did suddenly die in camp. We were told he had committed suicide, but we all knew that there was not a chance in the world he'd kill himself. That night the six of us, including your *baba*, made a secret pact. We would never kill ourselves under any circumstances. We'd fight to live, believing that in the end the truth would prevail."

Uncle Lu stopped again. He reached up to grasp the second button on his uniform. "We all agreed that if any one of us was about to be killed," he continued, "he would tear off this button from his uniform to let the others know the truth about his death."

Here, Uncle Lu paused, lost for a brief moment in his own memories.

"Oh, I am digressing," he said with a sigh, bringing himself back. "On that New Year's Eve, no one talked at all. Our tiny room was full of the smell of cheap cigarettes and the sounds of congested coughs. It must have been almost midnight. 'Enough,' your *baba* suddenly said, standing up. You know how soft-spoken he is, but he was unusually stern that night. 'We may not have a choice about how we die, but we do have a choice about how we live. We'll *not* pass into the new year with our spirits crushed. Look, we have all these wood chips on the floor. Let's try to make chess pieces out of them.'

"We lifted our heads. Like a small, efficient army, we all picked up a few wood chips and, using our pocketknives, started to carve them with our old hands. Soon, thirty-two rough pieces emerged. We wrote a character on each of them while someone drew a chessboard on a large piece of paper. And so we played chess well into the new year."

I was not surprised by Uncle Lu's story. It was just like my *baba*.

∽

Since he came back from the labor camp, I had tried not to pry into Baba's experiences there. I knew he would tell me when he was ready. And I was right.

A week after his return, Baba asked me to go for a walk with him. There was a small lake not far from where we lived. There was not much to it other than a replica of a wooden pagoda, a few willow trees, and a reassuring tranquillity. I came here of- ten—sometimes with friends, other times with Lao Lao. Occa- sionally Di Di and I fished here, just like we had in our movie studio days, even though we had never caught anything. More recently, however, I came alone, finding the serenity comforting.

Baba and I walked slowly around the lake, trying to soak in the last rays of warm sunshine before night took them away. "I have something important to confide in you," he finally said.

I now realized this was not a casual walk.

"Remember Uncle He?" he asked.

Uncle He, Baba's friend, was an army general. Even before Baba was taken away, I had heard that Uncle He had been se- verely beaten—with both legs broken—and he had been locked up in one of the high-security prisons. No one had seen him since, and no one knew exactly where he was or even whether he was still alive. His two children had been sent away to labor camps.

"Uncle He's wife came to me secretly the other night," Baba continued. "She was desperate—in very poor health and she feared not only for her husband but for her children. She didn't know where to turn. Even old friends have pretended not to know her. I went to Aunt Lin and borrowed two hundred yuan, of course not telling her who it was for, and gave the money to Mrs. He. This is *your* money, I told her, and you don't owe me anything.

"Now," Baba said, looking me in the eye. "I owe Aunt Lin two hundred yuan. You know, I will probably be taken away again soon, and there is always a chance I may never come back. You are my firstborn. I know you are only sixteen, but if I fail to return, I'll have to depend on you to repay the debt on my behalf. Would you promise me to do that?"

I stopped walking, even stopped breathing for a few moments. Two hundred yuan was more than half a year's salary for many city people. But Baba, I understood, was counting on me. Looking up at him, I nodded—*yes*. There, by the lake, I knew I had come of age.

湖南木乃伊

Hunan Mummy

ABA WAS SENT BACK, AND ANOTHER YEAR PASSED BEFORE HE WAS GRANTED A SECOND TEMPORARY RELEASE FROM THE LABOR CAMP. DURING THIS visit, in the province of Hunan, where our ancestors once lived, a sensational archaeological discovery was made.

In the spring of 1972, at the construction site of a hospital in Changsha, the capital of Hunan Province, the workers accidentally struck a large hidden tomb. As archaeologists rushed to the site, they unearthed a four-layered sarcophagus. The wooden coffins were covered with masterful oil paintings, their colors intact. The second layer was the most breathtaking, depicting a celestial scene with more than a hundred legendary fairies and animals floating amid white clouds.

Surrounded by over a thousand treasures—*zhubo* (bamboo strips and silk with rare ancient classics written on them), a twenty-five-string *se* (ancient Chinese harp), lacquered screens, and rare herbs—was the body of a fifty-year-old female from

200 B.C.: a two-thousand-year-old mummy! Newspapers reported that she was clothed in the finest silk—as thin as a cicada's wings and as light as vapor. Later, two other tombs were discovered next to hers—smaller but nonetheless impressive.

Who was this woman? people asked. Speculations and rumors circulated widely among our news-deprived population. "A national treasure of our motherland" was the official statement. "This mummy is proof that the technology of ancient China had no equal in the world. We are proud of our cultural heritage." Of course, the official paper continued, the discovery also demonstrated how the ruling class had robbed common people in order to enrich themselves—even after death.

Soon after this discovery, Baba invited his friend Uncle Li home for lunch. Uncle Li was one of the best photographers in China. He had been summoned to take official pictures of the Hunan Mummy, as the female body came to be called. Recently, he had returned to Beijing, full of stories—*unofficial* ones. I was all ears.

"They've opened up the mummy," Uncle Li began eagerly as soon as I carried a large bowl of spicy noodles to the table, "and they have taken out her heart, brain, and lungs—all fresh, as if she died yesterday—and put them in several jars of white liquid to preserve them for eternity."

I put down my chopsticks, losing my appetite completely as I visualized the organs resting in big jars.

But Uncle Li was full of excitement. "Can you guess what they found in her stomach?" he asked.

I shook my head.

"Sweet melon seeds!"

I was puzzled, but Baba explained, "In those days, sweet melons were brought to Beijing from the south, thousands of miles away, as tributes to the Emperor."

"That's right," Uncle Li continued. "But for the Hunan Mummy to have eaten these melons means only one thing—she was of imperial status."

I was intrigued; I had been following the story pretty carefully. The woman, Xin Zhui, as reported in the newspapers, was the wife of Marquis Li Cang of Changsha, a prefecture of the newly unified kingdom of Han. She certainly had status, but not *that* kind of status.

"Well," Uncle Li said, his eyes twinkling as if he had read my mind, "many believe that she was a favorite consort of one of the Han emperors, and had given birth to a son who became the heir to the throne. The Empress generously adopted the baby but secretly ordered Xin Zhui killed. The officer entrusted with carrying out the order took pity on Xin Zhui, and instead of killing her, he set her free, saying, 'May heaven protect you.' "

So far this sounded like the Snow White story I had read, albeit a Chinese version.

"The unfortunate woman drifted on the Xiang River for days," Uncle Li continued, "death chasing her like a shadow. She hid behind tall reeds, away from suspicious eyes during the day, and only traveled at night. Her will to live must have burned strong in her, like an undying fire, sustaining her through thirst, hunger, and many starless nights.

"As destiny would have it, she was finally rescued by a local farmer, who brought her home, nursed her back to health, and generously shared with her all that he had. In gratitude, Xin Zhui married the farmer. The couple lived on the fruits of their labor and raised their own family." Uncle Li took a sip of the jasmine tea.

"Years passed," he went on. "Finally, her imperial son ascended to the throne. The now elderly assassin, on his deathbed, confessed the truth to the young Emperor, who in turn immediately dispatched his Imperial Guards in search of his birth mother. It did not take them long to locate her, and a tearful reunion ensued. The Emperor, however, could not bring Xin Zhui back to the throne as Empress Dowager. Instead, he bestowed on the farmer husband the title of marquis, as well as a sizable land grant. He also lavished on his mother all the treasures of his court, including silk and sweet melons from down south. Upon her death, the Emperor gave her an extravagant imperial burial, complete with all the finest things from his Han kingdom.

"They have discovered two small tombs close by," Uncle Li added, "and believe that they belonged to her husband and their son. This seems to confirm the story, since both tombs were much smaller than Xin Zhui's. In feudal China, a wife could never have had a bigger tomb than her husband unless, of course, she had imperial connections." Uncle Li leaned back, his remarkable story finished, as I dished some more spicy noodles into his rice bowl.

Then, Baba surprised me with this revelation. "Our genealogy record from Hunan makes it seems likely that Xin Zhui was our ancestor."

"What?" I was stunned.

"You mustn't tell anyone!" Baba warned me. "We've had enough trouble with our family's political history without adding an ancestor who 'robbed the poor to enrich herself,' as the government claims."

I thought about Xin Zhui's farmer husband. He was once poor, right? Maybe we could focus on his proletarian past instead.

Not long after Uncle Li's visit, Baba was ordered back to his labor camp. I couldn't stop thinking about him and our newly found ancestor. If the story was true, I was grateful that Xin Zhui had fought hard to survive. Otherwise none of us would have been here. But now, Baba was battling for his life, too.

∽

With Baba gone, Uncle Li visited us frequently during the holidays, always bringing fresh fruits and new stories. Each time he came, I begged him to take me with him on his next trip to Hunan. "After all, I have to pay respect to my ancestor."

"Someday," he'd say, "someday." Uncle Li never did take me there, but I have not forgotten about Xin Zhui.

Years later, after she was put on display at the Hunan Provincial Museum, I finally had an opportunity to pay her a visit. It was a dreary, drizzling day, and the museum was nearly empty. As I stepped into the large exhibition room, I found myself alone with my two-thousand-year-old ancestor.

Gingerly, I approached Xin Zhui. She looked so small in that glass box, wrapped in a white cloth from contemporary China, her pale silk gown lying listless in another display box nearby. She looked as if she was in a deep sleep, oblivious to all the hoopla her discovery had caused. Her hair, thicker and darker than mine, looked a little disheveled. In her day, I imagined, she or her maids would have smoothed it out in front of a bronze mirror. I wondered how she would have reacted if she managed to wake up and find herself here on earth again—her body exposed, her loved ones gone.

I have heard a few other versions of Xin Zhui's story since that afternoon when Uncle Li regaled Baba and me with his vivid tale. Each of these reports is compelling and has its own dramatic details. But in the end, I still prefer Uncle Li's account. To me, it is a story about a life well lived—with adventures, highs, and lows. It is a story about a voice that stubbornly refuses to be silenced, and about a soul that, aided by good fortune, reinvents itself down the Xiang River on an ordinary farm, with an ordinary farmer. It is about a woman who, defying all odds, lives to tell her tale.

I believe Xin Zhui would have been happy without her featherlike silk gown or her imperial connection, as would anyone given a second chance in life. It is in Baba that I see a glimpse of her indomitable spirit. And it was in this spirit, as I stood in front of her, that I hoped we were related.

命運无主

A Life Assigned

NE FROSTY MORNING IN JANUARY 1973, I HUD-
DLED WITH MY FRIENDS BY THE OLD SCHOOL
GATE FOR THE LAST TIME. OUR TEACHERS, SOME
of whom had become closer to us than our parents during the
past tumultuous years, were too choked up to speak as they tried
to shake the hands of all of their "children." Dusty trucks pulled
into our gate, and one by one, we climbed onto them. From the
back of our truck, I leaned over, trying to hold on to my friends
one last time, feeling numb from both the cold weather and the
sadness deep inside my heart. At eighteen, I was being sent off
to face a new life—one that I had not chosen.

At our language school, classes had been suspended and
resumed a few times since the beginning of the Cultural Revolution. Then, in 1971, the school was transformed into a voca-
tional high school for language teachers—a profession all of us
were now ordered to enter. By then, most students and teachers
had returned to campus, and classes resumed. After years of

chaos, most of us were ready, even eager, to get back to some form of normality. I was grateful that this career transformation had, at least, spared us from being dispatched to the remote countryside of Inner Mongolia, as my cousin Lee had been. I had also grown to love the joy and fulfillment reading brought into my life. Baba's reading list and my secret reading club had rekindled my desire to learn. For the first time since the Cultural Revolution had begun, I felt I had regained some balance and direction in my life.

At school, we were once again allowed to read some classics in addition to Mao's work. Shakespeare and Mark Twain were still not encouraged, so we read Gorky instead. A loyal friend of Lenin and an acclaimed Soviet writer, Gorky, together with some of his revolutionary countrymen, provided a bit of nutrition as assigned reading material.

But, just as calm seemed to be returning to schools nationwide, an official evaluation of the educational system, initiated by members of what later came to be known as the Gang of Four—the chief architects of the Cultural Revolution—became public. Education, they claimed, was still controlled by bourgeois intellectuals. In contrast to what the Party endorsed, these intellectuals encouraged individualism instead of communalism and put book learning ahead of ideological training. Following the publication of this fateful paper, the teaching profession came under fire again, and in many schools across the country students walked out of their classrooms once more.

Here we were, teachers-to-be, trying to get ready for our

new mission while a fresh storm was raging around us. Quite a few of my classmates, including my best friend, Wen, chose to leave school to become soldiers. The army was still held in high esteem because of the endorsement by its supreme commander—Chairman Mao. The whole nation, it seemed, was madly in love with the uniform.

With his thin, tight face that never seemed to smile, Feng, our new head teacher, only aggravated the problem. "Our Party has *ordered* you to become teachers," he told us during his first assembly appearance. "Any reservation you hold is proof of your selfishness. It shows that you are putting your own interest ahead of the country."

Coming from a peasant family that had been poor for many generations, Teacher Feng claimed to have a spotless political background. A large red Mao button was always prominently pinned to the upper left pocket of his threadbare blue jacket.

Being in our late teens, and having experienced changing political winds much of our lives, we were no longer so easy to manipulate. Every few days, a student would disappear from class to join the army, making Teacher Feng frustrated. And frustration motivated him to resort to tactics accumulated during many of his successful political campaigns. "To subdue the bandit," he informed us, "one has to capture its ringleader." One of the "ringleaders" he targeted was Mei, a soft-spoken student of German and president of her class.

One evening we were called to attend a special assembly, without being told what it was about. Once everyone was seated and silent, Teacher Feng rose to his feet and ascended to the podium. From that vantage point, he surveyed us from left to right, creating suspense as he glanced at everyone in the room.

"We have a very sad case at hand," he said, carefully letting every syllable drop into the silence. "A class president betrayed our trust by failing to report that her mother had recently been classified by her company as an escaped enemy of the people. On top of that," Teacher Feng went on, raising both his voice and his finger, "this same person has expressed her dissatisfaction with the Party's decision to turn our school into a teachers' training school." He paused to assess our reaction and then asked, "How could a former student leader make such mistakes?"

My classmates and I looked at one another, wondering what would happen next. Eyeing Mei's best friend, Teacher Feng signaled her to stand. With a prepared speech in hand, the girl stood up slowly, her face pale and tense. Now everyone turned toward her. Lowering her head to avoid eye contact with anyone, she recited Mei's alleged wrongdoings in a shaky voice. After her speech, there was complete silence.

Then, at Teacher Feng's prodding, another student from Mei's class hesitantly rose. He stood there but said nothing for what seemed like an eternity. Finally, Teacher Feng stepped down from the podium and marched over to stand next to him. With the teacher towering above him, the student finally mumbled something and quickly sat back down.

This was only the beginning. The next morning, several big

posters appeared in Mei's classroom, denouncing her. Watching this drama unfold, I was shaken, not so much by Teacher Feng's manipulation—by now I had witnessed many skillful political maneuvers—but by the apparent willingness of Mei's friends to betray her. It had been one thing to watch from a distance as some adults sold out their friends for political gain; it was quite another to witness the same behavior among classmates and friends.

What was it, I asked myself, that made one person respond to the same threat or temptation with courage, while others reacted with fear and treachery? This incident made me even more aware of how vulnerable we all were.

The army looked more and more attractive to me now, since it seemed the only way I could avoid the chaos in education. When Baba came back for his temporary visit, I begged him to help get me in. But because of his unresolved political problems, Baba said, the army would not accept me. Unfair, I cried out. Since both Baba and Mama had joined the army when they were younger than I was, shouldn't the army take our family legacy into consideration?

Higher education, something I wanted with all my heart, did not seem possible. This was true for Di Di, too. At his school, he was initially on the short list for college. But after the school sent someone to Baba's movie studio to check on his current political status, they scratched Di Di's name from the list. At sixteen, he was assigned to work as a typist for the Ministry of Telecommunications. I knew my fate would not be any different.

And so, grudgingly, I found myself sitting in the large auditorium with over two hundred other students on graduation day. There was no ceremony, no donning of hats and gowns, just another long lecture from our new headmaster about the noble profession we were about to enter. Sitting on my wooden chair in the crowded hall, I passed the time playing tic-tac-toe with my equally bored friends, as we waited for our future to be decided for us.

Our names were read one by one from a long list, together with the names of the schools to which we were assigned. I was appointed to an international school, not too bad an assignment compared with those of some of my classmates, since having foreign students on campus would guarantee me a cleaner environment and a functioning heating system—China cared a lot about how it presented itself to the world. Unlike us, my future students would, at least, not have to wear mittens to class while they tried to take notes. Our final assembly ended as unceremoniously as it began, and we dragged ourselves back to our dorm to pack for an early departure the following day.

A wise friend once told me, "If you must leave a place you've lived in and loved, where all your yesterdays are buried deep, leave it fast and don't linger." There were certainly enough temptations for me to linger here; after all, I had lived most of my formative years at this school. But that world of yesterday, like my childhood, was gone. I had long ago stopped second-guessing the future, for fear it would turn out to be even more disappointing than all the broken dreams of my past. I tried to live each day as it came.

There was a feeling of absolute finality the next morning, when I climbed onto the truck and we pulled away into the gray haze that engulfed the city. I could almost smell in that wet, frosty air the end of a chapter in my life. As I rode across Beijing toward my assigned school, the journey—through the boisterous morning commute, cutting right through Tiananmen Square—was silent for me. The birds must have chirped, but they had no song I could hear. Instead, a hundred things—memories from my childhood—flashed through my mind.

I thought about Uncle Wang and Purple Cloud, our adopted foal, who together taught me about sharing, and about the pain and joy of a new life being born. I thought about the tadpoles swimming in our porcelain washbasins. I thought, too, about our old headmaster—his smashed glasses and his suicide note. And I missed my friends. Ten tumultuous years had gone by since fate had brought us together at the language school. Today, all these friends were heading toward their own assigned schools across the city, while I was on my way to mine.

Our truck made a silent turn, and the driver gave his horn a gentle, rhythmic tap, as if to bring me back to reality, before coming to a full stop at the International School. In front of me, a bright green wooden gate was slowly opening—to my new destiny.

日　壇

Temple of the Sun

URING THE NEXT FIVE YEARS, WHEN I TAUGHT AT THE INTERNATIONAL SCHOOL, I STROLLED INTO THE NEARBY RITAN PARK—THE PARK OF THE Temple of the Sun—every day at the break of dawn. As the sun chased away dark shadows and lit up the elm trees one by one, I could see shimmering dew on the petals of pink carnations and yellow chrysanthemums, and magpies flying from treetop to treetop in search of their breakfast. This was a time I felt the park was talking to me through its silence, sharing with me its memories and its secrets. These were the moments that the park became mine.

Ritan was once a majestic imperial garden, built after Beijing was designated the capital of the kingdom of Ming, some five hundred years ago. Within the master design of the capital city were four major imperial temples, representing the most important signs of the zodiac—the sun, the moon, heaven, and earth. The Temple of the Sun, Ritan, on the eastern side of the city, was a mirror image of its sister park to the west, Yuetan, the Temple of the Moon.

It was a simple park as imperial gardens went, but its simplicity had a powerful majesty. Shading the temples and the sidewalks were tall elm and oak trees that had observed the passing of many emperors and the transformation of ancient dynasties to the current republic. I liked to touch these silent trees, their roots spreading deep in the dark soil. I could almost feel life vibrating through their solid trunks. These were lives strengthened by solitude, and they had witnessed millions of other souls much more fragile and transient than their own.

At the center of Ritan was a white granite altar. Built as an open, flat surface on top of nine flights of stairs, the altar lay bare and unadorned under the sun. Here, for over four hundred years, the emperors came to worship the sun god at the spring equinox. Many feet since then had stepped onto it. The stone platform, standing in between heaven and earth, received everyone—kings and queens and common people—with equal respect, offering them a panoramic view of the park and, with some imagination, part of the zodiac it represents.

Surrounding the altar were acres of grass and pine trees, a recent addition. Under the shady trees and behind well-trimmed bushes were wooden benches, providing ideal meeting spots for young lovers and restful places for the weary. To me, the park was a shelter and a friend. It had also become my spacious backyard—a perfect place to revive an old habit. At boarding school during the pre–Cultural Revolution days, all of us had gotten up

The sun altar at the Temple of the Sun

early each morning to review our language lessons, reading them out loud while strolling around the school yard. Now, after a seven-year interval, I resumed the habit.

So as the sun rose, a few hours before I had to teach, I would take the footpath lying in the center of the park—the one walked by emperors on their way to the sun altar. There, I'd flip open my manila folder and start to read out loud while slowly strolling along. I made up my own textbook with loose-leaf papers—filled with passages copied from my favorite authors.

A quiet path at the Temple of the Sun

Along the way, I would run into a few fellow early birds, almost always the same elderly people. We would give a silent nod to one another without breaking our pace. Some of them would stop to practice *taiji*, or tai chi—their movements blending naturally into the rhythm of the waking day.

One morning, I was distracted by a silver-haired elderly man dressed in a *taiji* outfit. I remembered seeing him before, but today, as he practiced *taiji* in his flowing white silk garment against the background of a stately oak tree, he looked like someone from another time. I was no master of *taiji*, but his movements, deliberate and graceful, touched me. I smiled, and—breaking out of his *taiji* concentration—he smiled back.

"I am sorry, I didn't mean to disturb you," I began to apologize.

"No disturbance at all." He smiled again, this time speaking English. "I'm glad you've stopped by. I've listened to your reading a few times and liked it. I hope you don't mind." He sounded like a native English speaker.

"Are you an English professor?" I asked, surprised.

"I've taught occasionally, but before my retirement I was an English language editor at the Commercial Press," he replied. "That seems such a long time ago."

An editor. His English must be perfect! An idea flashed through my mind, but I was too timid to express it.

"I live close to the park," he volunteered. "You're welcome to visit me and see if there are some books you might like to borrow." I wondered whether he had read my mind. "Come after work today if you have time," he added, jotting down his address on my folder. "I'll introduce you to my family." With another exchange of smiles, we parted as naturally as we had met.

I have always wondered about the thin line separating chance from destiny. Or is there really a thin line after all? How can the course of one's life be altered by a smile exchanged or a word spoken on a footpath in a park forgotten by time? If I had not gone to the park that morning, or if I had never been assigned to the International School, would we ever have met? I had no answer. I could only wonder.

I went knocking on the door of the white-haired English editor as soon as school was over. His home lay on the other side of the park, shaded by the same aged elm trees. It was a small courtyard house, solid yet unassuming, home and shelter to three generations of a gentle and harmonious family.

Mr. Hu, my new friend, and his wife of fifty years lived in the house on the north side. Across from them was the family of their married daughter. The old couple shared a small bedroom and a larger study that reminded me of my parents' house—it was lined with bookshelves from floor to ceiling. I walked over to these bookshelves as soon as I entered the room and ran my fingers across familiar names—Dickens, Shakespeare, Mark Twain, Hemingway, Melville.

Watching me, Mr. Hu said, "You're welcome to any of the books in this house." From my *baba*, I knew that all book lovers were protective of their collections. To offer to lend books was the highest form of generosity. I was touched, and I told him so. Then, gathering my courage, I asked, "Would you be willing to accept a student?"

"I was hoping you would ask" was the unexpected answer. I looked from him to his wife. "My husband has told me about you," said Mrs. Hu, "even though we did not know who you were. He is very impressed by your discipline and tenacity, and he said you must have studied English with some excellent teachers."

I blushed and told them my short history. "Since I have no chance to further my education in college," I confessed, "I have to try to teach myself. By reading out loud in the park and committing to memory what's in front of me, I am doing the best I can."

I also admitted that I felt a real sense of urgency to improve my English. At the International School, many students were children of the staff at foreign embassies in Beijing. To some, English was their native language, even though most of my first graders could not yet read or write. My own exposure to English had been interrupted so many times by political turmoil. I needed to find a way to improve my language skills quickly. I had prayed for a teacher to guide me again.

That day, Mr. Hu and I agreed to meet every Friday afternoon. "Write a page on a topic of your choice," he said, "and we'll start from there." With this assignment, I left him and hurried back through the park to my school.

I soon found out that writing a meaningful essay in a single page is not easy. I tore up many pages before finally committing to one, using my freshly acquired typing skills and the brand-new typewriter from the school to squeeze it into a single-spaced page. It was about my first swim in the ocean.

Mr. Hu looked at my paper quickly during my second visit. "I'm going to be very strict, if that's okay with you," he said. "I will pick out all the problems with your writing, big and small. This time, I'll have you take your essay back and try to correct the mistakes yourself. That's the best way to learn. But let me show you how you can do it."

I took out my notebook.

Mr. Hu continued, "First, go over the content to be sure it makes sense. Then look at the grammar before moving on to spelling and punctuation. Separate your task each time you review the essay, and focus on only one issue at a time."

Very soon, our weekly tutoring went beyond my simple essay as we wandered through our lives—his well lived and mine just beginning. Through these conversations, I found out more about Mr. Hu.

Before coming to Beijing for college, he had been trained in a missionary school in Shanghai, established by the American Baptists in the late nineteenth century. A talented man, gifted in both music and language, he had to decide which one to pursue further after college. He eventually chose languages because of the realities of his life. His new bride had just announced to him that she was pregnant, and the prospect of raising a family narrowed his choices overnight. So he packed his music scores in a large box and moved his bride and their meager worldly possessions into a one-bedroom apartment provided by the Commercial Press.

Mr. Hu was not a man inclined to look back in regret; he believed every skill provided enjoyment through the process of perfection. And he was good at perfecting his skills. He became, in much less time than it took his peers, the senior English editor of the press, leaving his name and talent on an impressive list of translations—from the Bible to Shakespeare, from Dickens to one of the most respected Chinese-English dictionaries.

A decade later, in the early 1930s, when he finally moved his expanding family into this small courtyard, he bought himself a gift—a used upright piano. Dusting off his music scores, which had faded with the years, he felt he had at last brought together his two loves.

When the Cultural Revolution started, Mr. Hu had already been retired for many years. Retirement spared him from working on the farms, as most of his younger colleagues were forced to do, or from losing his books in a house search, but it did not release him from much else. His early history in the missionary school was targeted, and he was ordered to write confessions about how he had been brainwashed by the Americans. Not inclined to bitterness, Mr. Hu would shrug off these memories whenever the subject came up and move on to something more positive.

On his large desk and on top of his piano were piles of shoe boxes. Curiosity got the best of me one day and I asked what the boxes were for, since they were given such visible positions in the study. "I've been working on a new dictionary of English phrases," he admitted, "and I use those shoe boxes to store my notes." He opened up a box to show me. Stacked one after another in alphabetical order were index cards with English sayings on one side and Chinese on the other. There must have been hundreds in each box. They were remarkable notes.

"Look at this. It's one of my favorites." Mr. Hu picked up a card, like a child showing off his preferred toy. "'Time and tide wait for no man.' What a wonderful saying! How would you translate that into Chinese?"

When I hesitated, he flipped over the card and showed me his version, which not only perfectly captured the meaning but shared the same cadence. "Finding the best translation is like discovering a treasure," he said, turning the card back and forth to admire both versions.

"How long will it take you to complete the dictionary?"

"More than twenty years. Maybe you can help me someday."

I ran some simple calculations in my mind. Mr. Hu was already seventy-five years old. He would have to live to be almost a hundred in order to finish the dictionary. Somehow that thought bothered me more than it bothered him. From his perspective, it was all part of his life's work—work that he loved. I left his house that night still repeating to myself, "Time and tide wait for no man."

During another visit, Mr. Hu said to me, "Writing is like composing. There is usually a beginning, a transition, a recapitulation, and a finale." Then he sat down at the piano and demonstrated it to me. "Start with your essay from the very first line, like setting up the tone and melody of a piece of music. You have to be able to attract your listener's attention with a good opening; otherwise, some people won't have the patience to continue. Then smoothly transition to the next level. With practice, you will find your rhythm. Recapitulation is like reiterating the first statement, except with more complexity and refinement, and the finale should be like a bang, short but effective."

For five years every Friday, I hurried to my tutor's house—eagerly looking forward to sitting down with Mr. Hu under the soft light in his study while his wife poured us tea. My *baba* was back at the labor camp again. Even though Mama had been allowed to come home, she was not reinstated as dean of students. Lao Lao tried hard to make ends meet, but even her garden—my favorite childhood hangout—looked deserted, since for years no family gathering had taken place. I had decided to board at my school to avoid the daily commute. Now, it was sad going home.

The warmth and peace at Mr. Hu's made me feel at home again. There, the familiar guardians of the house—volume after volume of books—patiently kept us company. At Mr. Hu's, I was free once again to browse through these old and new "friends," and choose a special volume to bring back with me.

Like Baba, my tutor spoke in a soothing voice—ready to engage in any subject of my choice. I felt that he was carrying on my *baba's* role in his absence—guiding me on a quest for education when schooling was denied to me. I enjoyed being both a teacher and a student at the same time. During the day I stood behind the podium helping my young apprentices grow and learn. At night I became an eager student myself, absorbed by the magic world of knowledge revealed to me through the generosity of this kind man.

Ritan Park provided me with a physical refuge of peace and tranquillity. Mr. Hu and his family offered me another sanctuary—the sanctuary of education. In this safe haven, I was finally given a road map, with highlights on all the scenic routes that had been obscured from my vision. Each time one of my essays went through a professional polish by Mr. Hu, I felt an increased appreciation of the beauty of language and a deeper understanding of the meanings of words.

At my tutor's, I felt alive again—alive with a sense of mission and a sense of direction. Chance? Fate? I did not know and I did not care. I simply wanted to take in every word he said and every piece of advice he offered. I was ready.

覺醒

The Awakening

HE YEAR 1976 BEGAN AND ENDED LIKE A LONG, TRAGIC SAGA. WHEN THE HISTORICAL CURTAIN FINALLY SHUT, IT CLOSED ON THE LIVES OF THE most dramatic players on the stage of twentieth-century China—Chairman Mao Zedong, Premier Zhou Enlai, and Marshal Zhu De. For almost a century, these powerful figures had dominated the Chinese scene, changing the country's history forever. This fateful year stayed in my memory as a series of shock waves. By the end of it, I felt as if I had lived through several lifetimes packed with unexpected events—all of them earthshaking, and all of them very sad.

On January 8, in the dead of winter, I got up early after spending a warm and welcoming night at the home of my youngest auntie. Outside her fifth-floor apartment windows, frosted by the icy wind, the day was just breaking. Reluctantly, I closed the door behind me and fastened the top button of my dark blue winter coat. Covering most of my face with a yellow woolen shawl, I braced for the penetrating chill. The wait at the station, mercifully, was not too long before a commuter bus turned the corner and made its way toward me. I joined the early birds climbing up the steps of the gray bus, then slouched down in a seat near the door and closed my eyes, trying to make the best use of the hour-long ride.

As I was drifting off to sleep, the droning sound of a passenger's handheld radio woke me up. Annoyed by the disturbance, I shifted in my seat. But the deep, slow music caught my attention. It was funeral music. Who had died?

"Our beloved Premier Zhou Enlai passed away from late-stage cancer last night" came the somber voice of the announcer. I froze in my seat. No one on the bus said a word until the muffled sobs of an old woman two seats behind me broke the dark silence. Then the slender body of the young woman next to me began to shake uncontrollably, and an old man in a faded black coat buried his head in his arms and started weeping. I covered my mouth with my hands, as if death had invaded my body as well.

Feeling suffocated by the heavy sadness around me, I got off before my usual stop, trying to clear my thoughts by cutting through Ritan Park. Judging from the ease of their walk and the steadiness of their pedaling, most of the people I passed had not heard the news. The sky was a pervasive gray, and the sycamore trees lining the embassy district, their branches stripped naked by the ruthless winter, seemed drained of life. I hastened toward the temple, my faithful refuge—to think, to calm down, to breathe.

The death of Premier Zhou touched something deep in my

heart that had been dulled during the past ten years of end-less political infighting. The Cultural Revolution, allegedly initi-ated to break the old order, had shattered *all* order on its long march. Its casualty record read like the *Who's Who* of modern China.

At the top of this list was Liu Shaoqi, the former president of the People's Republic and Mao's right-hand man, who had died alone after years of public humiliation and physical torture. There was the poet-warrior Marshal Chen Yi, the second for-eign minister of the Republic, silenced by the pain of cancer and a broken heart while in captivity. Another of the ten marshals, the flamboyant He Long, died of a suspected insulin overdose at an army hospital, with his heart stopped but his eyes open. Even Mao's handpicked successor, Marshal Lin Biao, who had become the Chairman's faithful shadow during the past ten years—al-ways with Mao's Little Red Book in his hand and a Mona Lisa smile on his face—died in a plane crash in the cold desert of Outer Mongolia, after an alleged failed coup to usurp the chair-manship before his time.

Like a galaxy of shooting stars, the heroes of the People's Republic fell one after another. In this country of hero-worshippers, Zhou had been our last hope. To me, he repre-sented a rational voice in an irrational world, a lonely pillar of strength in a collapsing coliseum. After Mao, the hero of all he-roes, had undermined his own stardom with the inevitable fail-ure of his Cultural Revolution, most of his former worshippers, including me, had pinned their faith on Zhou. His dignity and elegance as the Premier had won China the respect of many nations.

As I walked along, the Temple of the Sun, as always, helped clear my mind. When I got to my school, it was still half asleep. Usually, I loved this quietness, but today I sat down at my desk with my class notes in front of me, unable to do a thing. Hong, a close friend and fellow teacher, was the first to join me, her eyes swollen. Within half an hour, more teachers arrived, and we comforted one another with our shared sadness.

"Let's hold a memorial service," someone finally said, breaking the silence.

"I'm not sure we're allowed to do that," our headmistress answered. "We've just received word from the Police Bureau that demonstrations of grief should be avoided, especially in places with a foreign presence."

Our school had been assigned a security officer from the Police Bureau, someone we all regarded as a lamb in wolf's clothing. Every day he would pace around the school a few times, chatting with teachers and other staff. The worst situations he had to handle were traffic jams at the school gate. Today, however, the lamb turned into a real wolf. The smile he had always worn on his face disappeared when he walked into each office informing us of the new instructions from his boss.

"No open demonstrations, no meetings," he announced.

"What can you do if we have one?" one of the young teachers teased him.

The answer was simple. "I'll arrest you," he snapped.

The day passed in tension and confusion. After school, a group of us got together to try to figure out what to do. "I heard flowers and wreaths have appeared at Tiananmen Square," said Tan, a French teacher. "People are defying the government's orders in Zhou's memory."

We headed for our bicycles. Tiananmen Square was only half an hour away. As we got closer, more and more people were crowding the road. Looking at the Monument to the People's Heroes, which stood five stories tall in the center of the square, I saw that over a dozen wreaths had been placed high up along its railing. Someone put a tape recorder in front of the wreaths, and funeral music filled the square.

"Why did you leave us, Premier Zhou?" a white-haired man demanded, pounding his chest. "What can we do without you?" His voice was soon overpowered by louder and louder sobbing from those around him.

"We have to do something at the school," said Hong. "What's wrong with having a memorial service? Is that really illegal?"

ᔕ

I gave up trying to sleep that night and, at five in the morning, hurried to my office. Hong and Tan came in soon after, their eyes still swollen.

"There are more flowers and wreaths in Tiananmen Square," Hong reported.

"And some people have hung their poems and other writings on the wreaths, too," said Tan. "Let's go to the headmistress and demand a memorial service."

The three of us doubled our pace up the two flights of stairs to the headmistress's bedroom. A youthful-looking woman in her mid-fifties, our headmistress usually presented herself well, with tailor-made jackets in fine wool, professionally pressed pants, and well-shined boots. She always stood out in a crowd. Today, when she opened the door, I was shocked to find her looking like an old woman.

"I have no authority to give you permission," she said. "But believe me, I am with you."

"Fine, we'll just say we did this without your permission," Hong said.

The headmistress looked conflicted. We, however, were full of resolve.

"I remember seeing Premier Zhou's portrait at my parents' house," I said. "I'll go and get it."

By the time I returned with the black-and-white photo, Hong and Tan had rounded up other supporters and were busy arranging a classroom for the occasion. I placed Zhou's picture on top of the teacher's podium, and another teacher put a white, handmade paper flower in front of it. There was no one orchestrating the situation, but our group worked efficiently. Soon the room was ready. "We've notified everyone to be here at six o'clock this evening," Hong said. We all nodded and then parted.

The memorial service was already packed with people when

I finally freed myself from my students. Looking across the room, I saw sadness, defiance, loss, and pain. "We've gathered here on our own to remember our beloved Premier," Hong said. "Let's begin." Then she sat down, unable to utter another word.

Tan stood up and walked to the podium, pulling out a small piece of paper. She began to read: "Premier Zhou, you are still with us. Just listen to the voices here and in Tiananmen Square . . ."

Several other teachers got up and read poems and essays written for the occasion. I felt my heart become lighter with the emotional outpouring. The security officer appeared toward the end of the ceremony, but he remained quiet.

$$\backsim$$

If some people had been silent at Zhou's passing in January, by April they were ready to let their voices be heard. On April 5, Qing Ming—Chinese Memorial Day—thousands of people poured into Tiananmen Square. Many of them brought wreaths made of fresh flowers; others pinned their poems and essays along the railings of the monument. A black-and-white portrait of Premier Zhou, ten feet tall, was placed at the center of the monument as if to witness this unprecedented occasion. Even the presence of the police and the threat of government sanction and jail could not stop us.

China was slowly awakening. Its long slumber had dulled its mind and numbed its limbs but did not steal its spirit. Over a million people from all around the country gathered that day in Tiananmen Square in memory of Premier Zhou. Like the scenes etched onto the marble relief of the monument, where one fallen hero was succeeded by the rise of another, on that day China saw millions rise after one hero fell. Those standing tall around the monument realized that, instead of hero-worshipping, they needed to become heroes themselves. Looking around me, I experienced the old pride I'd felt as a child walking along this central avenue, and, like the others present in the square, once again I lifted my head high.

∽

Then in July, an earthquake leveled the mining town of Tangshan, about ninety miles from Beijing. Shaken out of my sleep by the tremors, I ran to join others in the yard. The rest of the night passed in relative peace until several aftershocks and the alarming news of casualties broke that hot summer morning. Quickly, most of Beijing's residents moved their beds out into the streets, setting up temporary shelters at a safe distance from the buildings.

My *di di*, now a messenger with a motorcycle from the Ministry of Telecommunications, searched our house for rations and blankets. Then, on his own, he drove to Tangshan to volunteer his help. The eyewitness account he brought back was heartbreaking. Not one building was left standing in the city. Many bodies that had been crushed under cement floors remained visible from the streets. Even in parts of Beijing, older buildings crumbled during the numerous aftershocks. "We are being punished for something this year," people said.

∽

The punishment did not stop with Zhou's death or the earthquake. Less than two months after the tragedy in Tangshan, Chairman Mao himself passed away. For over half a century, he had dominated the Chinese consciousness. Now reactions to his death were mixed. For many of us, looking around at the broken pieces of our lives, our unquestioning trust in this godlike figure had disappeared. Some people turned faith into hatred. Others felt lost, while many were simply suspended in frozen disbelief. Unlike the day when Premier Zhou died, I had no tears left for Mao. But all of us agreed that the passing of Chairman Mao marked the end of an era.

One day, a month after Mao's passing, Tan pulled me aside. "The Gang of Four have been arrested," she whispered. Her parents, former colleagues of Premier Zhou, had shared the news with her. "I'm going to tell Hong."

"Be careful," I warned. "It has not been made public." Then I left for home myself to share the unannounced news with my family.

Before nightfall, however, I heard a nervous knock on the door. It was Hong. "Tan has been arrested."

"Arrested? When?" I was stunned. "Who betrayed her?"

"It must have been the headmistress," Hong said. "Maybe she overheard our conversation about the Gang of Four."

"We must call Tan's parents and warn them," I said. I dialed their number, but no one answered.

I spent another sleepless night, worrying about Tan. But news of the arrest of the Gang of Four was broadcast the next morning, and Tan was released. The mood among the teachers, however, turned from shock to anger—anger at the headmistress.

"It's time we teach her a lesson about betrayal," many said. "What if the Gang of Four's arrest had only been a rumor? Then Tan would have been in real trouble."

I ran straight to the headmistress's office. In the past, I had considered her a friend; she had always encouraged my studies and had shared stories of her family's suffering during the Cultural Revolution. How could she betray one of her own teachers?

"Why did you do this to Tan?" I demanded.

She broke down in tears as soon as I began my questions. "She was on the Police Bureau's watch list. And I was ordered to report her every move."

"How could you? Your family suffered, too!"

"My family did suffer," she said, lowering her head, "but as the head of a school under the scrutiny of the Police Bureau, I had no choice."

I knew she was telling the truth, but I was still angry.

When I walked into the cafeteria at lunchtime, posters demanding her resignation were everywhere. It was like experiencing the Cultural Revolution all over again. Several teachers called a meeting that afternoon to confront her. I went with them but kept silent. The headmistress was obviously wrong, but the tone some of the teachers took reminded me of Red Guards at my high school—they were out for blood.

Soon after the incident, the headmistress was transferred to another school. I stood at the window of my office watching her disappear behind the walls, thinking about all that had happened and feeling conflicted about her fate.

Never before had I experienced a year like 1976. And never in my wildest dreams could I have imagined that this eventful year would become a turning point in my life.

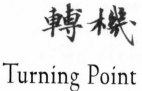

Turning Point

FTEN DURING THE PAST TEN YEARS, I HAD FELT LIKE A SAILOR STRANDED IN SHALLOW WATER, WAITING DAY AFTER DAY FOR THE TIDE TO RISE and the wind to blow. In the meantime, I had been fixing my vessel and studying my charts to make sure that when my chance came I would be prepared.

Then the wind changed. In 1977, for the first time in ten years, a national examination system for college enrollment was put in place. During the Cultural Revolution, the only qualification most colleges were allowed to use was that their candidates came from working-class backgrounds, narrowly defined as factory workers, farmers, and soldiers—so most of my friends and I had been immediately disqualified. Now I was turning twenty-three, the age limit for my school of choice, Beijing Foreign Language Institute. There was no time to waste. I filed my application as an English major.

To apply as a language student, I had to take entrance exams in Chinese, history and geography, English, mathematics, and politics. For me English would be easy, and so would Chinese. I would need to brush up on geography and history. As for politics, the most boring of all the subjects, I left reviewing it to the very end. Math was my biggest challenge. Most of our math instruction had stopped at fifth grade. Now that we were facing college entrance exams, grade school math was obviously not enough. How could I prepare myself in time?

Two math teachers from the International School came to my rescue. They volunteered to teach me and the other four college candidates from our school. We crammed in as many calculations and formulas as we could possibly absorb.

The few months that followed were filled with the most intense studying I had ever done, occupying every waking minute. I felt as if I had been living all these years for this one, final moment. Like a marathon runner with the finish line in view, I fixed my eyes on the thin line that would separate my past from my future.

In December 1977, the first day of the exams arrived. The examination hall was a few miles away. Several teachers walked us to the end of our street to cheer us on. Then, ready for battle, we mounted our bicycles and charged toward our destiny.

Politics was the first test. I sweated out the three hours without lifting my head. When we finally walked out of the exam room, three of our colleagues were anxiously waiting for us. Together they escorted us back to our school. There, we found fruit, candies, warm tea, and many friends, as if welcoming soldiers back from the front line. The next few days passed with mounting intensity and fatigue as I struggled through the rest of the exams, including the dreaded math test—only to be followed by what felt like the longest wait of my life.

Then, finally—good news. All five of us got in! For me, the door had opened to my first choice—the Foreign Language Institute.

When I brought the news to Mr. Hu, he was so happy that he immediately asked his wife to prepare a big dinner to celebrate and then spent the rest of the afternoon playing the piano for me. I had never seen him so pleased. Before I left, he put his treasured copy of *The Oxford English Dictionary* into my hands. It was worn from years of careful use, and on the title page he'd written in beautiful calligraphy, "To my young friend, with respect."

The next day, Hong, my friend from the International School, insisted on taking me to the only fancy "Western" restaurant in Beijing—the Moscow Restaurant—to celebrate. Sitting under its high ceiling decorated with crystal chandeliers, and looking at the starched white table linen, I felt like I was part of a private coronation. As we raised our glasses to toast the occasion, I noticed two young men next to us. Their large table was covered with expensive dishes; none, however, had been touched.

Curious, I said hello to them and introduced Hong as well. Then I asked, "Is everything okay?"

"Not really," one of them answered, sighing. "We've both just failed to get into any university."

Hong and I joined our table with theirs. Slowly they told us their story. "We've been working on a farm for the past five years, toiling like animals day after day. When they announced the new enrollment system, we tried to study every night under kerosene lamps, hoping to catch up. But we were just too far behind. Since we're already in our late twenties, we've just lost our last opportunity for college. We came back to Beijing to beg some school to give us another chance, even though we knew in our hearts that it was unlikely. This is our 'last supper.' We are failures."

Hong and I tried our best to console them, but none of us ate much of our Russian food. Walking out of the Moscow Restaurant, I lost all my feelings of self-congratulation and gained a new sense of humility. In college, I vowed, I would study hard for myself—and for both of them.

∽

My first day of school finally arrived. That morning, I got up earlier than usual. Lao Lao had already been in the kitchen cooking breakfast for me. On the dining table were fried eggs, dumplings, pickled cabbage, steamy porridge, and fresh bread. "Who else is coming for breakfast?" I joked, putting my arms around her.

After breakfast, I put on my favorite maroon jacket, hand-washed and ironed by Lao Lao the night before, and jumped onto my bicycle, looking forward to the long ride to school. On this early spring day of 1978, the Beijing sky was a turquoise blue. I breathed in the crisp air as the magpies, perching on top of the elm trees that lined our streets, chirped their songs.

The entrance to the Foreign Language Institute was wide open, inviting students directly into the administrative buildings. Hua, another childhood friend of mine, met me at the English Department, a big smile on her face. "You're in my class!" Almost choking her with a bear hug, I felt nine years old again—back in the days of our language school.

Arm in arm, we walked into our classroom. The majority of the students in my class came from the two former language schools in Beijing. As a result, I felt like I was part of a long-awaited class reunion. Looking around, I could not help but experience déjà vu—the stiff wooden desks and chairs, the high teacher's podium, and the spartan-looking room. Today, they all felt like the dearest things on earth to me. Ages seemed to have passed since my classmates and I last sat together. Now, as adults, we were finally reunited.

To our class, the school assigned the best professors they had—from Canada, New Zealand, the United States, as well as a few of the finest graduates from our own institute. Our curriculum, all required, included English and American literature, linguistics, sociology, Chinese, and politics. During the first month, we spent a few class hours on the Declaration of Independence, many of us reading it for the first time. I was both intrigued and impressed by the egalitarian ideals of the American Founding Fathers, whose modern descendants had become our country's enemies. Most of us also tried to commit to memory the Gettysburg Address, by an American president with an admirable background, who rose from being a self-taught farmer to become the leader of his nation's fight against slavery.

To supplement our class material, we raided our impoverished school library. I headed for the shelves with their dusty volumes of Shakespeare, a thinner collection than Mr. Hu's. One day my heart leapt when I discovered, at the bottom of a bookshelf in the far corner of the library, an old anthology of speeches by Winston Churchill, who had been introduced to me with great admiration by my tutor. I had only read two of his speeches before but had never forgotten his determined voice announcing to the world that Britain was ready to fight in the fields and in the streets, and never surrender. I brought the book back to my bedroom, laid it next to my pillow, and read it when I first woke up in the morning and just before I turned off the light at night, like a child rewarding herself with precious candies. I was in heaven.

But my heavenly experience at the university lasted only a short year and a half. Suddenly, the head of the English Department asked a few of us to his office. "You've been selected to change your white student badges into red teachers' badges," he announced. "A rare honor."

After ten years of educational poverty because of the Cultural Revolution, universities all across China were starving for young professors. Many of them decided to choose some current students to use as faculty. Although I was honored to be selected, somehow I felt deprived. Every day I had relished my hard-earned student life. Was it over forever now?

The answer to this question came unexpectedly one night not long afterward. As I was just about to sit down in the school cafeteria for my simple meal, Ning, an old classmate from the language school, followed me to the table. In a hushed voice, he asked a surprising question: "Would you like to study in America?"

China had only recently resumed diplomatic relations with the United States. Few people I knew had any firsthand knowledge of this former enemy. It was not long ago, I remembered, that we had marched to protest America's invasion of Vietnam.

"A friend of mine is an American professor here in Beijing," explained Ning, "and has asked me to recommend a few students to study in the U.S." Then he cautioned, "We have to do this without the school's knowledge, of course, just in case. Would you like to meet him?"

I said I certainly would.

The next day we bicycled to Beijing Teachers' College for my first meeting with the American professor, a Chinese-American man my age.

"Greetings," he said in Chinese with a thick American accent. "I'm Justin Kee." Justin was a third-generation American whose grandparents had emigrated from Guangdong Province. Soon after his graduation from Harvard University, Justin told me, he had eagerly accepted this teaching position in order to come back to his ancestral land.

"A few American universities have asked me to recruit students from China for them," he said. "I'd like to know if you are interested."

"Yes," I answered. "But how could I afford it?"

"These universities are giving full scholarships to qualified candidates, and I'd be delighted to help you try."

It sounded too good to be true, and Justin read my mind. "Where there's a will, there's a way," he assured me.

Not long afterward, I met with Justin again, this time with two other students from my college. One of them was my friend Hua, whom I had convinced to apply with me. This time Justin handed each of us several bulging application packages. During the next few days, Hua and I locked ourselves up in our bedrooms and started our application process. Her father had bought her a small typewriter in Hong Kong some time ago, and we put it to good use, filling in our application forms and typing up our required essays. In secret, we asked three of our trusted professors—including our lead teacher, Professor Su— for recommendations, and they bravely accepted. Hua and I told no one else what we were up to. Keeping secrets was not hard after our experiences during the Cultural Revolution.

Then came the long wait. I tried not to get my hopes too high, even though, deep down, I was overwhelmed with excitement. Finally, on a sunny late spring day, I heard a knock on my door. It was Justin—with a small envelope in his hand and a big smile on his face.

"I told you, where there's a will, there's a way!"

I had been offered a full scholarship to Swarthmore College near Philadelphia—the City of Brotherly Love. My two friends were accepted into other schools. A brand-new door was opening up into a world that was both exhilarating and foreign.

But a few days later, that door seemed to be closing once again when Professor Su came to see me. "I'm afraid something has gone terribly wrong," he said, still panting from climbing the stairs. "The secretary I had asked to type your recommendations became frightened and reported everything to the school authorities," he explained. "The school has called an emergency meeting on Sunday."

"What?"

"I'm worried," he said. "They could use you as guinea pigs to scare off others from applying to colleges outside China."

Quickly, I went looking for my other friends. The four of us, including Ning, met at a deserted corner of the campus.

"I'll talk to the dean," volunteered Jin, the third person in our secret group. "And you two go and beg the other professors to help."

We decided to meet again at dinnertime. Immediately, Hua and I went to see Professor Xu, a well-respected authority on English literature.

"What can they do to us?" we asked him.

"It's very hard to tell, but the worst could be expulsion," he told us.

"My God!"

"I will certainly talk to the president on your behalf," said Professor Xu, "but I just don't know whether he is in a position to help. His hands are tied, too."

We left our professor with even heavier hearts. For us, tomorrow would bring either the promised land or permanent expulsion—making it impossible to leave the country. For without written permission from the university or an official work unit, the Police Bureau would not issue anyone a passport. That night seemed to go on forever, and I could not close my eyes. At midnight, I gave up trying, put on my clothes, and went out of the dormitory.

The spring night was crisp and quiet. The college had become as familiar to me as an old friend. Even the dark silhouettes of the monotonous buildings, with their uniform gray color, were comforting to me. Along the college's walkways, I had practiced my English every morning at dawn together with hundreds of other students. There, my friends and I frequently put up our homemade net to play badminton after class. During the summer, the outdoor swimming pool was my favorite spot. And I could always find a quiet corner on this busy campus to listen to radio broadcasts of the Voice of America or the British Broadcasting Corporation. For the first time in ten years, there appeared to be a growing sense of academic freedom, as well as a heartwarming camaraderie among fellow students. Here, finally, I felt at home. Was I going to be forced to throw all this away in just a few hours?

I looked around the campus and walked the familiar, well-shaded roads again, until the last few lights were dimmed. Tired and a little resigned, I finally returned to my room.

The next day Hua and I got up early. The campus was nearly empty, with students gone for the weekend. We collected our laundry and washed it together by hand under the cold tap water, as we had done every week for the past two years. Half a day passed; the tension we felt increased with each passing hour. Finally, we were summoned to the president's office. I had always liked the president—a calm old man with a warm smile. Today he was calm but not smiling, and he came right to the point.

"The school wants the three of you to go home and ask your parents to write us their opinion of what you have done. Then we'll decide what to do with you." Surprised by the simplicity of the demand, we left for home.

After hearing my story, Baba laughed. "The school just wants to have a written record from someone at a higher political level so that they know where to shift the blame if something goes wrong." But of course, I thought. Jin was the son of a powerful senior government official. Our school would follow whatever direction his father indicated in his correspondence.

With a brief note from Baba supporting my efforts, I went back to school. Jin came back with a letter signed by his mother, which read, "My son is twenty-one years old now, and I believe he is mature enough to choose his own future." As my father had guessed, that fateful letter reopened the door to the promised land. I would be among one of the first groups of Chinese students since 1949 to study in America.

ဢ

The weeks that followed became a blur, with farewell parties hosted by family, friends, and classmates. There was no direct flight from Beijing to the United States, so I had decided to take the train to Guangzhou and then to Hong Kong, where Pan Am would take me to the West.

My whole family and many friends came to see me off at the Beijing Railway Station. Baba, finally home for good from his labor camp in Shanxi, made sure everyone was cheerful, as if I was merely leaving for boarding school again. I tried my best to cheer up Lao Lao. At seventy, she was still a picture of elegance and grace. Age had been kind to her, even though life had not. For the occasion, she put on a new light blue silk blouse and a pair of matching pants. Her hair, highlighted by some silvery strands, was combed back carefully and tightened with a black hair band I had bought for her at a local market. I held on to her arm while walking toward the train, as I had done all my life—leaning on her for security, comfort, and love.

When I finally stepped onto the train that would take me to the southern border of China, Lao Lao reached out and put a small package in my hand. I held her hands until Wen and Mama finally persuaded us to let go. Di Di and my other friends waved as they walked alongside the departing train. Through the open window, I took one last good look at my loved ones.

At fifty, and finally free from many of the nightmares of the past decade, Baba and Mama were poised for a second spring. Di Di was a first-year student at my university. My best friend of seventeen years, Wen, had become a head nurse at her army hospital. Now, both her hands were in the air, waving to me. When the train started to pick up speed, I saw Lao Lao pulling out her handkerchief to wipe away her tears. All of a sudden, I was seized by a gnawing loneliness—just like that day when I was nine and had sat on my bed alone at boarding school. What would be waiting for me in America?

Then I remembered Lao Lao's little package. Eagerly, I peeled away the paper wrapping and uncovered a small, red velvet pouch. Inside was a gold necklace with Lao Lao's first name, Zhen, meaning loyalty, carved in the center of the pendant. Trying to fight back tears, I ran my hand over the heart-shaped locket, which she'd worn through many happy and sad days. Would I ever see her again?

∽

My last night in China I spent in Guangzhou. I tried, but failed, to close my eyes and quiet my mind. I lay there for hours thinking—about the sunlight and the shadows, the songs and the sorrows. My country had suffered, and I had suffered with it. China was the land that had given me birth, love, and friendship. It was also the place of my darkest nightmares. People would judge it in different ways. Some would appraise it kindly; others would be harsh. To me, however, China was simply home—the breath and life of my childhood and of my youth.

The next morning, I stepped off the Hong Kong–bound train and stood at the border between the mainland and the British colony. I knew that even though China would be there forever, as it had been for thousands of years, it would never be quite the same to anyone who left it.

To cross the border into Hong Kong, all travelers had to

walk over a hundred-year-old passage called Luohu Bridge. There were pushcarts on the mainland side. I loaded my two bulging suitcases onto one. Taking a last look at the land I had called home for twenty-six years, I put my shoulder to the cart and joined the silent and slow-moving crowd. It was time to cross the bridge.

Epilogue

As I am putting the finishing touches on this memoir, twenty-six years have passed since I left China for America. By now, I have lived in both worlds for exactly the same amount of time. To help refresh my memory, I went back a second time to the site of our old courtyard in Beijing.

On that early spring day, an unseasonable snow was falling, but I could see golden daffodils peeking out through the frozen ground. Sitting there once again among the shattered bricks, I felt the past awakening in my mind. There, in the safety of my memory, nothing could be taken from me. And there, I was home again.

A Chronology

1976	January	Premier Zhou Enlai dies.
	April	Riots occur in Tiananmen Square, Beijing.
	July	Marshal Zhu De dies.
		An earthquake destroys Tangshan.
	September	Chairman Mao Zedong dies.
	October	The Gang of Four are arrested.
		The Cultural Revolution officially ends.
1977		The national entrance examination for college resumes for the first time in ten years.
1979		The United States and the People's Republic of China establish full diplomatic relations.

Glossary

baba Father.

changpao Traditional gown, robe.

Chiang Kai-shek (1887–1975) Leader of the Nationalists, the Kuomintang (KMT), from 1928 to 1975. After the Nationalist troops retreated to Taiwan, he remained President and Director-General of the KMT until his death.

Chinese Communist Party (CCP) A political party founded in 1921. It became the controlling party of the People's Republic of China in 1949.

Cultural Revolution (The Great Proletarian Cultural Revolution) A political movement initiated by Mao Zedong that lasted from 1966 until 1976. It was characterized by political zealotry, purges of intellectuals, and social and economic chaos.

da jiu Oldest maternal uncle.

dazibao **(large-character poster)** A form of propaganda in the style of a large handwritten poster. During the Cultural Revolution, *dazibao* was used to attack and disgrace people.

di di Younger brother.

Gang of Four Four leaders held responsible for the excesses of the Cultural Revolution. The most notable of the Gang of Four was Jiang Qing, Mao's widow. The others were Wang Hongwen, Yao Wenyuan, and Zhang Chunqiao.

Great Leap Forward An industrial and agricultural campaign undertaken between 1958 and early 1960. The programs were implemented so hastily and zealously that many mistakes were made. A series of natural disasters and the withdrawal of Soviet technical personnel compounded these mistakes, causing China's agriculture to be severely disrupted, and widespread famine occurred from 1959 to 1961.

hongweibing (see **Red Guard**)

huaishu Scholar tree.

huanying Welcome.

hutong Narrow streets or alleys, most commonly associated with Beijing.

jin A unit of weight, slightly heavier than a pound.

jiu jiu Maternal uncle.

kang A heatable brick or clay bed with a hollow center, so that heat from an adjacent room (usually a kitchen stove) can travel through and heat the bed.

lao lao Maternal grandmother.

lao ye Maternal grandfather.

Little Red Book Pocket-size edition of quotations from Chairman Mao.

Mao Zedong (1893–1976) A founder of the Chinese Communist Party in 1921, he led the People's Republic of China from 1949 until his death. As Party chairman and the country's first head of state, he initiated the Great Leap Forward and was a leading figure in the Cultural Revolution.

Nationalist Party (Kuomintang, KMT) A political party founded by Sun Yat-sen and his followers in 1912 and led by Chiang Kai-shek from 1928 to 1975. It has been the dominant party of Taiwan since 1949.

People's Daily An official newspaper of the Chinese government.

People's Republic of China After a bitter civil war (1946–49) between the Nationalists, led by Chiang Kai-shek, and the Communists, headed by Mao Zedong, a people's republic led by Mao Zedong was established on the mainland, and the Nationalists fled to Taiwan.

Red Guard Political units of university and high school students formed during the Cultural Revolution. Responding in 1966 to Chairman Mao's call to revitalize the country's revolutionary spirit, they tried to purge the country of its pre-Communist culture. With membership in the millions, many of them attacked and persecuted local party leaders, teachers, and other intellectuals.

Republic of China Established in 1912, this replaced the Qing Dynasty, ending over two thousand years of imperial rule in China. The Republic of China went through periods of warlordism, Japanese invasion, and civil war between the Kuomintang and the Communists. In 1949, the People's Republic of China replaced the Republic of China on the mainland.

se An ancient Chinese zither (string instrument).

sihai (**four evils**) Defined by Chairman Mao to include sparrows, rats, flies, and mosquitoes. In early 1958, the government waged a sanitation movement with the goal of eliminating these *sihai* from the country within ten years.

siheyuan (**courtyard house**) A type of residence commonly found throughout China, especially in Beijing. It consists of a yard surrounded by four buildings.

Sun Yat-sen (1866–1925) Considered the father of modern China. Educated in Hawaii and Hong Kong, Sun embarked on a medical career in 1892, but gave up medicine two years later for politics. He became the provisional president of the Republic of China from 1911 to 1912 after overthrowing the Qing Dynasty.

taiji Commonly known as tai chi, t'ai chi, or taijiquan, this Chinese martial art was originally an effective and powerful system of fighting. Today *taiji* is often practiced as a way of achieving good health.

tianzu The literal translation of the term is "heavenly feet." It was used by some in China to refer to women's feet that were allowed to grow naturally, as opposed to those that were bound in early childhood.

War of Resistance (1937–45) A major war fought between the Republic of China and the Empire of Japan, both before and during World War II. Although the two countries had fought intermittently since 1931, full-scale war started in 1937 and ended only with the surrender of Japan in 1945. From 1937 to 1941, China fought alone. After the attack on Pearl Harbor, the War of Resistance merged into the greater conflict of World War II.

ye ye Paternal grandfather.

yi yi Maternal aunt.

yuan A denomination of the official currency of the People's Republic of China.

zhichuang Shutters.

Zhou Enlai (1898–1976) Premier of the People's Republic of China from its founding in 1949 until his death. Zhou became a Communist while studying in France and was an organizer for the Chinese Communist Party in Europe. When the Communists prevailed over the Nationalists, Zhou became Premier. During the Cultural Revolution, Zhou helped restrain extremists and restore Deng Xiaoping and other moderates to power. He is credited with arranging the historic meeting between President Richard Nixon and Chairman Mao Zedong that paved the way for the normalization of diplomatic relations between the two countries.

zhubo Bamboo strips or silk cloth that people in ancient China wrote on before paper was available.

Zhu De (1886–1976) A military leader and statesman, he is regarded as one of the founders of the Chinese Red Army. After 1949, Zhu was named Commander-in-Chief of the People's Liberation Army. In 1966, he was dismissed from his position in the Standing Committee of the National People's Congress, but was reinstated in 1971.

zu ye Paternal or maternal great-grandfather.

Acknowledgments

ike life, no publication is a solitary journey. I am blessed with friends and family on both sides of the globe—China and the United States—who have helped shape and sustain me as much in life as in this creative process. I am reminded, constantly, by how each country has allowed me to better understand the other.

I would like to thank my Chinese and American families—some associated by blood, most by choice—for helping me create and comprehend my life experiences. To my parents, Baba and Mama, thank you for instilling in me the value system that has been my essence. Thanks to my aunties and uncles, for protecting me ever since I came into the world. To my brother, Di Di, thank you for sharing the happy and challenging days of our childhood. To my teachers and friends Hu Shuyuan and Chen Jianing, I am forever grateful for your guidance and instruction at times in my life when higher education was denied.

And to my dear friends of forty years, Huang Jianhua, Lei

Yan, and Xie Gang, thank you for your unwavering friendship throughout our lives and for helping me sift through my memory.

If my Chinese family helped shape my memories, my American family helped give them perspective. I would like to give my deep appreciation to Dr. Howard Rosenblatt: he and his family have adopted me as one of their own since I came to the United States, sharing their Passover seder with me. To Camille and Joyce Sarrouf, who have opened their house and their hearts to my husband and me—no Christmas, Thanksgiving, or Easter would ever be the same without them. To my other American brothers and sisters—Joe and Julie Phelan, Steve Andress, Debbie Kee, Phill and Liz Gross—thank you for your love and for your valuable feedback on my manuscript. To my friends and former professors David Hall and Alan Lawson, thank you for your insightful comments and for your friendship. To my friends Hualing Nie-Engel and Natasa Dovonolova, I am sincerely grateful for your careful reading of the manuscript and your astute observations.

My appreciation also goes to my mother-in-law, Kay Pease, and to my friends Susan Roosevelt Weld, Bill Frohlich, Lexa Marshall, Betty Lowry, Adrienne Richard, and Richard Harley. Heartfelt thanks also go to Wendy Strothman, my literary agent and friend—you are a dream come true to any aspiring author—and to my editor, Melanie Kroupa, for her wisdom, patience, and advice, and to the many others at Farrar, Straus and Giroux who helped create this book.

It is not an exaggeration to say that this book would not have been conceived or completed without my husband, Paul Marcus, who has urged me, from the day we met, to share my story with others. During the past twelve years of our marriage, he has helped me trim and shape each story, and it is his faith in my experience that has sustained me through the inevitable trials and unpredictability of this journey.